MY NAME ESCAPES ME

WITHDRAWN

MY NAME ESCAPES ME

The Diary of a Retiring Actor

Alec Guinness

with a preface by John le Carré

Thorndike Press
Thorndike, Maine USA

This Large Print edition is published by Thorndike Press, USA.

Published in 1998 in the U.S. by arrangement with Sinclair-Stevenson.

U.S. Softcover ISBN 0–7862–1203–9 (General Series Edition)

Copyright © Alec Guinness, 1996

The moral right of the author has been asserted.

'A Mission into Enemy Territory' by John le Carré is reproduced by kind permission of David Higham Associates.

Grateful acknowledgement is made to Faber & Faber Ltd. for permission to reproduce lines from *Four Quartets* by T. S. Eliot.

The text of this Large Print edition is unabridged.
Other aspects of the book may vary from the original edition.

Set in 16 pt. New Times Roman.

Printed in Great Britain on acid-free paper.

Library of Congress Cataloging-in-Publication Data

Guinness, Alec, 1914–
    My name escapes me : the diary of a retiring actor / Alec Guinness; with a preface by John le Carré.
        p. cm.
    Originally published : London : Hamish Hamilton, 1996.
    ISBN 0–7862–1203–9 (large print : sc : alk. paper)
    1. Guinness, Alec, 1914– —Diaries. 2. Actors—Great Britain—Diaries. 3. Large type books. I. Title.
[PN2598.G8A3   1998]
792'.028'092—dc21
[B]   97-24578

For Merula, of course

No Spring, nor Summer Beauty hath such
  grace
As I have seen in one Autumnal face.

JOHN DONNE

PREFACE BY JOHN LE CARRÉ

A Mission into Enemy Territory

He is not a comfortable companion. Why should he be? The watching child inside this eighty-year-old man has still found no safe harbours or easy answers. The deprivals and humiliations of three quarters of a century ago are unresolved. It is as though he were still striving to appease the adult world about him; to winkle love from it, to beg its smile, to deflect or harness its monstrosity.

But he loathes its flattery, and mistrusts its praise. He is as wary as children learn to be. He gives his trust slowly, and with the greatest care. And he is ready any time to take it back. If you are incurably fond of him, as I am, you do best to keep your feelings to yourself.

Form is desperately important to him. As someone all too familiar with chaos, he treasures good manners and good order. He inclines gratefully to the good-looking, but also loves clowns, apes and quirkish figures in the street, gazing on them as if they were his natural allies.

Day and night he studies and stores away the mannerisms of the adult enemy, moulds his own face, voice and body into countless versions of us, while he simultaneously explores the possibilities of his own nature—do you like me better so—or so?—or so?—ad infinitum. When he is composing character, he steals shamelessly from those around him.

After lunch with Sir Maurice Oldfield, a retired head of the British Secret Service, who was not Smiley but resembled him, Alec hastened out into the street to watch him walk away from us. Oldfield's orange suède boots, the quaintly didactic waddle, the clumsy cufflinks, the poorly rolled umbrella, were added to Smiley's properties chest from then on.

Watching him putting on an identity is like watching a man set out on a mission into enemy territory. Is the disguise right for *him*? (*Him* being himself in his new persona.) Are his spectacles right?—no, let's try those. His shoes, are they too good, too new, will they give him away? And this walk, this thing he does with his knee, this glance, this posture—not too much, you think? And if he looks like a native, will he speak like one—does he master the vernacular?

And when the show is over, or the day's shoot, and he is once more Alec—the fluid face shiny from the make-up, the small cigar trembling slightly in the thick hand—you can't help feeling what a dull old world he has come back to, after all the adventures he has had out there.

He may be a solitary, but the former naval officer also loves to be part of a team. He wishes nothing better than to be well led, able to respect the meaning of his orders and the quality of his comrades. Acting with them, he knows their lines as well as he knows his own. Beyond all self-consideration, it is the collective illusion that he treasures most, called otherwise The Show: that precious other world where life has meaning, form and resolution, and events proceed according to written rules.

Working on scripts with him is what Americans call a learning experience. One scene may go through a dozen versions before he is persuaded by it. Another, for no reason, is nodded through without debate. It's only later, when you see what he has decided to do with it, that you discover why.

The disciplines he imposes on himself are rigorous, and he expects no less of others. I was present once when an actor who has since become teetotal turned up drunk for filming— not least because he was terrified of acting opposite Guinness. The offence, in Alec's eyes, was absolute: the poor man might as well have gone to sleep on sentry duty. But, ten minutes later, Alec's anger had given way to an almost desperate kindliness. The next day's shoot went like a dream.

Ask Alec to dinner, he will be on your doorstep brushed and polished while the clock is still chiming the appointed time, never mind the blizzard that has brought London to a standstill. If you are his guest—a more likely eventuality, since he is a compulsively generous host—then a postcard, in neat and beautiful handwriting sinking gracefully to the south-east, will confirm the arrangement you made on the telephone the day before.

And you will do well to repay him the courtesy of his punctuality. Your gestures matter very much to him. They are a mandatory part of life's script, they are what distinguishes us from the indignity and disorder of his wretched early years.

But God forbid that I should paint him as a stern man. Alec's bubbling laughter and good fellowship, when they come, are all the more miraculous for the uncertain weather that preceded them. The sudden beam of pleasure, the marvellously paced anecdotes, the flashes of physical and vocal mimicry, the mischievous dolphin smile that spreads and flits away, are all before me as I write. Watch him in the company of fellow actors of every age and provenance, and you see him settle to them like a man who has found a favourite fireside. The new never shocks him. He loves to discover young talent and give it a helping hand along the hard road he has trodden.

And he reads.

Some actors, offered work, first count their lines to calculate the importance of the part. Alec is as far removed from them as it is possible to be. No film director, producer or screenwriter of my acquaintance has a better eye for structure and dialogue, or for that *extra something* that he is perennially on the scent of: the McGuffin, the bit of magic that lifts a piece out of the common ruck.

It is no coincidence that Alec's career is studded with brilliant and unlikely roles. The talent that chose them was as inspired as the talent that performed them. I have heard too—is it one of Alec's well-kept secrets?—that his wife Merula has much influence on his selections. I would not be in the least surprised. She is a wise and quiet woman, and a most gentle artist, and she sees a long way.

What joins us, then, those of us who have been lucky enough to share a mile or two of Alec's long life? I suspect, a constant bewilderment about who to be for him. You want to show him your love, but you want also to give him the space he clearly needs. His talent is so near the surface that your immediate instinct is to protect it from the buffetings of daily life. But then he can manage quite nicely by himself, thank you.

So we become like the rest of his great, audience: frustrated givers, never able to express our gratitude, reconciled to being the beneficiaries of the genius he so resolutely refuses to acknowledge.

A WORD IN YOUR EYE

Towards the end of 1994 Mr Charles Moore, who at that time was Editor of the *Sunday Telegraph*, took me to lunch and said that if I kept a diary throughout 1995 he would be prepared to make two or three selections from it for publication in the paper. I was apprehensive and flattered, and finally I agreed.

I have kept a diary for over thirty years; a small, strictly private, almost illegible series of daily jottings, and I have left instructions for them to be destroyed at my death. The only use I have ever found for them has been to settle arguments when my wife and I have disagreed about where we were, when and with whom, in years long past.

My Name Escapes Me is rather different, being fuller, quirkier and more haphazard and, to my regret, unavoidably self-revealing; which is something I hadn't bargained for. I have been unable to disguise my phobias, irritations, prejudices (though the latter are often short-lived) and my childishness and frivolity. Sometimes, I hope, my occasional enthusiasms emerge.

When I am asked, which is all too often, if I have retired, I am inclined to assume a pained expression and deny it. At eighty-two I am well past my sell-by date and I doubt if any part, however small, would tempt me. The difficulty is the chore of learning (I used to be reasonably reliable and fairly quick) and diminishing physical vitality, both of which would choke any creative effort. So I am happy to scribble instead.

My gratitude over this book goes out to many: to my wife, Merula, who hasn't read a word of it and who assumes, when I retire to my study, that I am doing serious work and not just frittering away time foolishly; to Miss Elizabeth Dove, whom I have driven to near distraction at her typewriter; to our friend and neighbour Mrs Blake Parker, who tactfully queries my spelling of words like Hezbollah or piranha by pretending she herself doesn't know; to Mr Christopher Sinclair-Stevenson, who shepherded me through my previous attempt at a book, *Blessings in Disguise*, and has given me a shove with this one; to Mr Tony Lacey of Penguin Books, who has shown no sign yet of the alarm he must feel; and to Mr John le Carré for giving permission for his brilliant, penetrating essay on my personality to be used as a foreword. Who could object to being referred to as 'an uncomfortable companion' when the writing is so beautiful and witty. Also my thanks must go to Dame Drue Heinz, who offered me asylum in her villa on Lake Como as my dreaded deadline came up.

2

The diary covers the period from January 1995 to early June 1996.

JANUARY 1995

Sunday 1 January

Through a chink in the bedroom curtains my unenthusiastic eye caught an early-morning glimpse of the New Year: it looked battleship-grey. As I reluctantly swung out of bed I noticed my feet—never something on which I like to dwell. They appeared to be crumbling, sandstone monuments, the soles criss-crossed with ancient, indecipherable runes, which probably hold the secrets of eighty years of living and partly living—of happiness and fears, of distresses, of rather embarrassing successes and expected failures. I drew open the curtains and found the sky was in fact a cloudless blue and the tops of the trees promised sunlight. It was all very different from exactly fifty-one years ago when I was wrecked in a hurricane in the Adriatic, chucked around by thirty-foot waves and a wind of 120 m.p.h. I never liked New Year's Day anyway; it has too often felt like a day of foreboding.

No resolutions have been made. Experience has taught me they barely survive a week. But I have made a few negative wishes for other people. I never wish to see again any reproduction of Andy Warhol's portrait of Marilyn Monroe. Also I am anxious about that elderly lady lying on her face at the bottom of her stairs, clutching the accident alarm which is meant to alert her neighbours. She has been prostrate there for about two years and still no one has come to her aid. And I long for twelve months when no politician will use the word 'clear' to describe what is manifestly muddy or incomprehensible. Would all BBC (and other) announcers please read and inwardly digest Robert Burchfield's *The Spoken Word*? It is slim, pocketable, authoritative and, after all, a BBC publication by a great lexicographer.

A sudden little blizzard made us too apprehensive to drive the couple of miles to Mass in the evening, so I threw a log on the fire and mixed a lethal cocktail called, I believe, the Claridge. (Half and half gin and French vermouth, with a good dash of Cointreau and apricot brandy.) That kept our eyes, slightly unfocused, on the TV production of *Cold Comfort Farm*.

Tuesday 3 January
We pray for peace throughout the world but I can't help rejoicing at the way the Chechen fighters are picking off invading Russian troops and knocking out their armoured vehicles. And yet the pity of it all; the Russians we see on the screen look like bewildered schoolboys, the Chechens alert and dedicated young men.

I am nearing the end of Volume 4 of the RLS *Letters.* Compulsive and, on the whole, delightful reading but I grow weary of Mrs Fanny Stevenson's constant diarrhoea and Louis's haemorrhages. (They both had the same difficulty in spelling these words as I have.) And to think that I, a Stevenson fan from an early age, have always referred to him as Louis (as in Quatorze) when he pronounced his name like the Hebridean island. I do hope they soon sort out their financial problems; the constant borrowing is embarrassing. It is time, 1883, he made big money.

I want their wayward Skye terrier, Wogg.

Wednesday 11 January
Bitterly cold. To London by car to give lunch to Ed Herrmann (American actor friend) who is only over here for a day and a night. We had a good meal at Neal's in Neal Street but had difficulty with our conversation because of the guffawing of five cigar-chomping American businessmen at the next table. Ed dropped his head in his hands and moaned, 'Oh, my fellow-countrymen abroad.' Dinner at a Fulham Road restaurant in the evening was pierced by the shrieks of pretty Sloane Rangers. I was a guest of Ronnie Harwood—always warm and entertaining—but the only words I'm confident I heard him say were Douglas Hurd, Lady Thatcher, Waldegrave, Albert Finney and veal.

To the National Portrait Gallery to see the Sitwell exhibition. I particularly liked Derek Hill's portrait of Sacheverell, painted in the seventies. It is a remarkable likeness; the eyes have a curious, fastidious and disapproving glint which I remember well. The Tchelitchew paintings of Edith seem to me to be striving after something other than the sitter; himself perhaps. Early in the war I had tea with him in New York; very agreeable, and camply amusing, but I had the impression I was in the presence of a professional exile—something I often feel about Russians or eastern Europeans. Edith's famous aquamarines were rather tattily presented and some of her clothes looked as if dragged from a dressing-up hamper—a facade and a charade. I miss her kindness and Plantagenet condescension.

Nancy Cunard's long long elegant feet in the painting by Alvaro Guevara, 1919, look like transatlantic liners.

Friday 13 January
Death has made some swift, unexpected and sad visitations since Christmas: John Osborne (who could be enchanting), Fanny Cradock and Peter Cook. All regrettable, but the theatre did *not* begin with *Look Back in Anger*, as we are so frequently instructed; Cradock's cooking appeared, to me, over-elaborate and ill-tempered; and Peter Cook's obituaries seemed to take up more press coverage than

would the assassination of the entire royal family. I asked Alan Bennett if he could account for it. 'He was a journalist,' he said.

Wednesday 18 January
A cheering day. M and I to London by car. In the afternoon to the Cromwell Hospital for M to be seen by the Spinal Disorder Unit. All is rather hopeful, or at least not catastrophic: a change of medication; she is to continue going for short walks and to return to the hospital in a month's time. When we got back to the hotel there was a telephone message from the Crane Kalman Gallery inviting M to contribute half a dozen pictures to the mixed show they are having in mid-February: a big morale booster. We ordered Buck's Fizz to celebrate. It had the look and scent of mimosa in Portugal in the early spring.

Tuesday 24 January
Death continues to claim my friends; three days ago John Kidd, an admirable actor of charm, great intelligence and absurd humility; and yesterday evening Fr. Derek Jennings, with whom I had become close friends in the past eight years. I met him first in 1984, before he was ordained; he was in the entourage of Princess Margaret at a performance of *The Merchant of Venice* in Chichester. 'You know Derek?' she asked in introducing him. I said I didn't. 'It's too awful,' HRH continued. 'He has become a Roman Catholic and now he

talks about becoming a priest.' Derek caught my eye and gave an amused, discreet shrug. I liked him instantly. He laughed easily. The Cardinal, who had been most kind during the six months of Derek's cancer and visited him on his sickbed, was with him at the moment of death. Not even the presence of the Pope would have given him greater pleasure. Too young to leave us, at forty-eight.

Merula and I spent Easter last year in Rome and as Derek was there we met up each day. He pulled a dozen strings or bishop's tassels, manoeuvring us into places or ceremonies we would not otherwise have seen. Then, in the early summer, we had a week together in the Dolomites; but although he remained outwardly cheerful, the disease was beginning to take its toll. He tired easily and became fastidious about his food. He said, quite brightly, he expected to die by Christmas.

More than anything else I think he taught me to trust Divine Providence and chuck away all notions of luck. Well, I go along with that these days; but I don't think Providence is in the least interested in my relationship with the National Lottery.

Sunday 29 January
Gave Irene (Worth) and Mu (Richardson) lunch at the Connaught; splendid roast beef and Yorkshire pudding. Mu and I were not drinking wine but Irene was so delighted with

her individual half bottle of Aloxe Corton that, when it was down to roughly two inches, she asked if it could be corked up for her to take home. I refused; but ordered another half bottle, which she took away wrapped in brown paper.

In the evening to the Savoy for the Evening Standard Film Awards, at which I received a special award (long service?) from the hands of the Duchess of Kent. I had been told I would be on, so to speak, at 21.45 so it was arranged I would be at the hotel by 21.15. Which I was. Already things were running an hour late. One recipient droned on so long with his acceptance speech that I nodded off. I saw no reason why he should ever end; perhaps he is still speaking—in his bath. Speeches sound better in a bath.

Sat next to Nicola Pagett, which was a comfort. The vast banqueting room was jammed full and hot. Richard Harris, at same table, wore a sort of piratical evening suit and had his hair in a fetching little pony-tail. He made a funny speech. Diana Rigg, looking stunning in black, made a charming but over-the-top citation about me. People were up and down and up and down to receive trophies for *Four Weddings and a Funeral*. The trophy is very handsome—a silvered version of Piccadilly's Eros. It could prove a lethal weapon for dealing with burglars if you could summon the strength to lift it. And if you dared the legal consequences of defending your own person and property. Will 1995 be the year of Universal Suing? Policemen, I read, are resorting to the courts because of the state of their nerves after the horrid things they have seen at football matches; and a lot of soldiers want compensation because they have discovered that war is beastly. Oh, Sceptred Isle set in the polluted sea, where are we heading?

FEBRUARY 1995

Tuesday 14 February
A Valentine card in a tiny illiterate hand; surely I can't have sent a card to myself. Now that Dr Alzheimer looks as if he may be extending a welcome to me I can no longer be sure of these things.

The radio travel news started, as it does most mornings, with information about an overturned truck on a main road. A tailback from here to eternity. A few days ago I drove past a lorry lying on its side, resembling some vast, incapacitated woodlouse. Blue and yellow lights were flashing all over the place and a small crowd had collected, laughing and excitedly chattering, as if a fairground was being set up. The ambulance siren could still be heard, receding.

Wednesday 15 February
Vicious violence at Ireland v. England soccer match in Dublin. English fans clearly responsible. I almost feel the nation is trying to commit suicide. And then I remember all the marvellous young people who give their services in desperate parts of the world and I take heart.

Tuesday 21 February
'Careful!' I said to Merula. 'That tall, smiling

young man side-winding towards you is a gossip columnist, if ever I saw one.' We were at the crowded opening last week of an exhibition at the Crane Kalman Gallery (Knightsbridge), where she had half a dozen pictures on display. 'What's more,' I said, 'I know the type. He'll be very agreeable but get everything just a little bit wrong.' But it wasn't Merula he struck at. Yesterday *The Times*, under a photograph of me as George Smiley, announced I had retired; which isn't exactly so.

In answer to his smiling questions I said I was unlikely to work in the theatre again (certainly not in the West End), that I find I enjoy not working and that No, even if asked, I wouldn't be appearing in any *Star War* sequels. So that, it seems, is retirement.

Today I have picked up a rather good notice in an American film trade paper for a performance I have never given in a film I have never heard of. It says that I am 'almost unrecognizable' in the film. I like the 'almost'.

The sky is cloudless, the wind cold, the crocuses have flopped over and the future of the daffodils looks doubtful. The ground is so wet that every step is a squelch. Moss appears to be replacing grass but there is a definite feel of spring in the air; which brings to mind an old song of Douggie Byng's.

Sunday 26 February
The amount of space in the papers given up to

14

Stephen Fry's defection from the Simon Gray play *Cell Mates* is astonishing. His reported faxed statements from the Continent have been somewhat elaborate, very apologetic and sympathy-seeking. Well, he will get all the sympathy he needs, I'm sure, for what is presumably a sort of breakdown; but I can't help feeling an actor should be made of sterner stuff. Most actors are as tough as old boots. As Shakespeare knew. 'After your death you were better have a bad epitaph than their ill report while you live.'

'What do you want to be when you grow up, Billy?'

'I hope to be an actor.'

'But, Billy, actors don't grow up. And you, Lancelot?'

'A drama critic.'

'Really? That's unusual. I hope you won't find it a bore after a year or two. And you, Penelope, if you ever grow up?'

'I'm going to be a director, a director, a director.'

'You always were a chatterbox, Penelope. Not one of you has said you want to be a playwright. How sad. All of you wish to put the cart before the horse.'

Monday 6 March
To the National Theatre for lunch given by Lady Soames at the Ian Charleson awards, handsomely donated by the *Sunday Times*. I was put between Lady S and Richard Eyre as I had to present certificates and large cheque prizes. It was all very painless. Top prize went to Maggie Smith's and Robert Stephens's son, Toby, currently playing Coriolanus. He is an enchanting and attractive young man, obviously destined to be a real ornament in the British Theatre. With such parents it is hardly surprising.

After lunch I taxied, through violent rain squalls, to the Sainsbury wing of the National Gallery to see the Spanish Still Life exhibition. Was almost miffed, when I asked for a concession ticket, that I wasn't challenged to prove I am a Senior Citizen; and how. The exhibition is a knockout. Paintings of great floral arrangements depress me and I skipped most of those, but the pictures of pots, pans, vegetables, fish and strung-up apples— particularly those by Juan Cotán—are breathtaking. Perhaps it is the almost geometric composition that roots one to the spot. Or the sheer blackness of Spanish black paint. I wanted to shout '*olé*'.

In the evening to Quentin Stevenson's flat in Kensington to collect him for dinner and to look at his remarkable collection of pictures— mostly from the beginning of the century until the late thirties and mostly by women. He is an admirable poet and as an actor is known professionally as John Quentin.

Came up to town yesterday (Sunday) afternoon and went to 16.15 Mass at Farm Street. The homily, by an American priest I think, was mostly inaudible and I was having difficulty in keeping awake through the interminable drawl when I was suddenly alert. From the pulpit I distinctly heard, 'And the serpent said to Eve, "Hi, Eve! Take a look at this bright red apple! Yum, yum."'

Dinner with Christopher and Debbie Sinclair-Stevenson; better than red apples.

Thursday 9 March
Anemone blanda begin to show.

An eager woman's voice invites us, in kindergarten tones, to listen this afternoon on BBC radio to 'a Russian play, "The *Three* Sisters"'. Not having heard 'The *Two* Sisters' (*Three* sounds like a sequel) I shall give it a miss. A friend swears that a few years back he heard an American woman, leaving the theatre after a performance of *Uncle Vanya*, say to her companion, 'I didn't enjoy it as much as "The Cherry Sisters".'

Tuesday 14 March
When British actors go to the USA to sell their wares and set about their lawful business, the press in New York, LA, Boston or wherever treats them with great courtesy. It is a pity that American performers visiting this country aren't welcomed in the same way. Many of them must dread the English experience.

Today's *Daily Telegraph* carries a full-page interview with Lauren Bacall which, for sheer unpleasant rudeness, takes some beating. Bacall, the widow of Humphrey Bogart and later the wife of Jason Robards, is twice referred to, in a jokey-snobby way, by her maiden name of Betty Perske. Good for a snigger perhaps? Of course Bacall is well able to take care of herself—with a straight left to the chin probably—but such action shouldn't be required of a lady over seventy.

Tuesday 21 March
The ornamental cherry tree outside my study, very gnarled, twisted and Japanese, is showing pale magenta blossom here and there. The larches appear to be in a slight green haze. A beautiful day, marred by a telephone call saying that Bobby Flemyng has had a serious stroke and is in a coma. He is one of my closest actor friends.

The night before last I dreamed that Bobby had died and much of yesterday I half expected to hear of his death. A dear, good man; always caring and conscientious; he has given so much of his life to others. The past few years have been made wretched for him with unsuccessful operations. I've never heard him complain, except lightly, for the sake of a laugh. He had very good timing. In the war he achieved the rank of lieutenant-colonel and was decorated for bravery.

My small world threatens to be underpopulated.

Thursday 23 March
Yesterday evening we watched Miriam Rothschild on BBC 2's 'Seven Wonders of the World' series and thought she was terrific— entertaining, vital and astonishing. But the programme was all too short—half an hour. I want it repeated, enlarged and for her to give hours more of her knowledge and wisdom. I want to know more (or at least I *think* I do) about the microscopic pond creature that can disappear up its own fundament; about the remarkable hopping of fleas; and about carotenoids, colour, light and sight. While she is about it perhaps she could expand on a report in today's *Telegraph* about the farting of termites. Apparently their farts are adding about 10 per cent to global warming. True? Or false? I think we should be told. They sound like rivals to Auberon Waugh's American hamburgers.

Saturday 25 March
> 'Doth the moon shine that night we play
>   our play?'
> 'A calendar, a calendar! Look in the
>   almanack;
> find out moonshine, find out moonshine!'
> 'Yes, it doth shine that night.'
>
> *A Midsummer Night's Dream*, III, i.

That bustling bit of dialogue obviously suggests a realistic approach. Why do actors and directors so often fantasticate the mechanics? Surely they are much funnier when presented as real people. It is the same with Feydeau farce; the hilarity lies in seeing dull, stodgy, ordinary bourgeois people caught up in improbable situations.

Looking at my own almanack I see that in the small hours tonight we have the biannual fiddle with clocks, and its weary wrangle about an hour forwards or backwards. Grounds for divorce. There is a certain amount of excitement watching our radio-controlled clock go berserk for a few minutes and then right itself as if nothing untoward had happened; an enviable disposition.

Tuesday 28 March
A touch of sleet and occasional light snow. Depressing. As was, I suppose, the Oscar news on the radio. I have seen none of the films or performances which were nominated, but I did

see Nigel Hawthorne in the stage version of *The Madness of George III* and thought him magnificent; I can't believe he would be less so on the screen. I hope he doesn't greatly care. It is the hype which has become so exasperating—and its inevitable let-down. Not much hype in 1957 when *The Bridge on the River Kwai* brought me an Oscar but the let-down was there sure enough. It was the *Daily Express*, I think, which carried a banner headline which read, 'Deborah Kerr fails for the third time'. A very English assessment. She hadn't failed in any real sense (she had several beautiful performances to her credit)—she just hadn't been handed a trophy. A race or a fight or a game can be won but to call something 'the best' in the arts is absurd. I wouldn't mind betting Dickens would fail to win the Booker Prize (too readable and too funny) and Turner the Turner Prize and poor Keats wouldn't even be considered for any poetry prize. And so on. I suggest that the givers of awards to actors, writers and artists should choose half a dozen, almost at random, and say, 'These are people we wish to honour—equally.'

Geoffrey Madan, in his *Notebooks*, quotes a Canon Liddon as follows: 'The applause of all but very good men is no more than the precise measure of their possible hostility.'

APRIL 1995

Saturday 1 April
To St Thomas's Hospital to see Bobby Flemyng. He can't speak but has a little movement in his left hand. His eyes suggested he recognized me and knew what I was saying, which was just self-conscious rubbish. Very difficult to say anything to someone who can't answer back; everything that came to mind was so banal or falsely cheerful. Shame drove me away within four minutes.

In the evening gave dinner to John and Teresa Wells and Alan B. The object was to either congratulate or console Alan on the Oscars outcome. To console as it turned out; but he said he preferred the caviar to any Oscar.

On Thursday I did my first-ever voice-over for, of all people, the Inland Revenue; a cartoon to reassure the public about the new tax forms which are to be introduced. The young men in charge of the recording were so laid back (on a vast semicircular sofa) that I doubt if they registered that I had come or gone. I did it feebly anyway.

On Friday I was offered another voice-over; this time for the Euro Tunnel. It so happens that two weeks ago I booked three first-class return tickets to Paris for 2 May. I was told that our Senior Citizen rail cards would knock £90 off each ticket. Lovely. But not so, it appears. This Friday I was informed that the train had its full quota of Senior Citizens for the day I am travelling. This is the first I've heard of such a quota. Will it soon apply to our Inter-City routes? I'm not doing the voice-over: though I would do so happily if they would allow me to warn other elderly travellers of this let-down.

Thursday 13 April
This is the eleventh day of sunshine; anyway in the south. Cherry blossom is softly brilliant and heart-touching. A lot of my time is being spent assisting indignant bumble-bees trapped behind window-panes: their bigness, noisiness and silliness is somehow appealing.

On Monday dined at the Garrick, sitting next to the painter Keith Grant. We chatted away for an hour, finding we had a shared enthusiasm for Iceland and an interest in Ruskin, Edward Lear, Lowry and Gwen John. He fired my longing to see again, before I die, the aurora borealis, that ever changing, breath-stopping, Wonder of All Wonders of the World.

Today's *Telegraph* carries an account of aborted human foetuses being sold in China for human consumption. Mostly used in soups, the article says, with just a touch of ginger. I'm not sure I shall be able to eat ginger again.

Last night watched TV documentary on Liz Brewer (who proved likeable and honest) and her work promoting wanna-be members of so-called Café Society. Much of it hilarious, particularly Ivana Trump. I think I can already hear the tumbrils taking the Brewer clients up Park Lane to Tyburn.

Monday 24 April
Over the weekend BBC radio announced a programme about 'Roodi-yard Kipling' and Mr Dimbleby, hosting his 'Any Questions', gave us '*lamen*table'.

To London to have a back tooth out; never felt a thing, but the tingling in my lips as the injection wore off was a subtle torture. I mumbled to the hotel linkman that I wasn't drunk. He gave a quizzical smile.

Went to the watercolour exhibition at Spink's, particularly to have a look at Ruskin's little picture of the 'Château of Neuchâtel at Dusk'. Wonderful dark blues, very Turneresque. Also I wanted to see Lear's 'Bethlehem', which proved not very interesting except for its date—2 April 1858, a Good Friday. Apparently he had moved out of Jerusalem because it was too crowded with pilgrims. And I have always been intrigued at what went on in the world on my birthdays long before I was born. Anyway I can't possibly afford either of them or the breezy 'Entrance to Plymouth Sound' by Nicolas

Condy. I dislike this covetousness in myself; but at least I have no desire for grand houses, smart cars or yachts. Of course all that could change at five past eight on a Saturday night when those dizzying little balls are released from their wire cage and the young cheer meaninglessly.

MAY 1995

Tuesday 2 May
To Waterloo International to Chunnel our way to Paris. (Merula, Marriott White and me.) Not a porter in sight, but we found a clever trolley that took to the escalator like a duck-billed platypus to water. There must have been about seven hundred people standing around in the departure lounge waiting to embark for France or Belgium. Our Eurostar was half an hour late in leaving, made a fitful journey through Kent (due to faulty signals at Ashford, we were told) and arrived at Gare du Nord an hour late. A gentleman seated with us informed me, as far as I could make out, that it was all the fault of Harold Wilson when prime minister. The train we found very comfortable and the sensation, if any, was of sliding over a frozen lake. No porters in Paris and hot.

The Lancaster Hotel very welcoming. Dined at Pierre au Palais Royal, an old haunt of ours; reassuringly good French bourgeois. The restaurant was empty, as were the streets. Taxis plentiful. Apparently the nation was glued to its TV sets watching the presidential debate.

Wednesday 3 May
Left from Gare de Lyon at 13.15 (half an hour late) on the Rapide for Avignon. A charming,

jolly porter sprinted off the platform and returned with an office chair to enable Merula to sit. A lovely train, when it did arrive, and the journey through a very green France kept us smiling for three hours. No porters at Avignon of course. Taxied to Villeneuve-les-Avignon to spend five nights at Le Prieuré. An admirable, very pretty hotel. We have a good large room with balcony overlooking the swimming-pool and shady gardens. The only tiresomeness is the hooting, every forty minutes or so, of goods trains as they burst their way in and out of tunnels quite near by. Otherwise it is all birdsong and beautiful intertwined plane trees, which let through just the right amount of dappled sunlight.

We have a vast spick-and-span bathroom. But why do the French provide such minuscule lavatories that you can barely shut the door on yourself?

Thursday 4 May
This morning we explored Villeneuve in hot sunshine and taxied to Avignon for lunch at La Fourchette (recommended by Le Prieuré and absolutely the sort of place we like—small, busy, friendly and with excellent unpretentious food). Under an adjacent table sat a West Highland terrier puppy, greatly cherished by his teenage boy owner, lapping water from an ashtray. We returned to Villeneuve in mid-afternoon and collapsed on our beds, always a

favourite occupation of mine. I have brought the new Le Carré to read, also *Antony and Cleopatra* and Homer's *Odyssey* in the Rieu translation. It is going to be too hot to cope with any of them. Oh, and certainly not Ruskin's *The Crown of Wild Olive*.

Friday 5 May
To La Fourchette again. We want to know how they do their black olive and caper spread, which seems as good as caviar. Our taxi-driver, Roger, is an exceptionally nice young man and looks like being a fixture during our stay. He took us to Orange immediately after lunch to see the Roman theatre, reputed to be the best preserved in the Roman world. A vast stage and an auditorium to hold about nine thousand. The dressing-rooms, if that is what they were, look tiny, airless and underground—rather like those at the Criterion.

This evening we dined in the hotel courtyard under the plane trees. A small party of very quiet, well-dressed Japanese arrived. One tall young woman, of striking beauty, was dressed superbly in a fawn-coloured suit of marvellous cut. Totally simple. It made everything you see in a Bond Street shop-window look like glittering vulgar trash.

Saturday 6 May
Hot but fresh and lovely. We set off at 11.20

(Roger's taxi) to see the Pont du Gard, a new sight for the three of us. Breathtaking. Built 19 BC. What architecture of ours will last so long? We walked across it in both directions, looking down a great distance to the blue and green of the river. A few small boys were splashing around from rocks and sandy beaches, looking like minnows. A tiny lizard fixed me with pinprick-sized eyes and when it thought I wasn't looking darted into a Roman crevice which looked smaller than itself.

We went on to Uzès to lunch with Patrick Woodcock at his attractive house in the middle of the town. I had only ever met him once before, but we have, and have had, a lot of mutual friends: Peter Bull, and the three Brown(e)s—Pamela, Irene and Coral—and Peggy Ashcroft and Leueen MacGrath. All sadly gone. He has been doctor and friend to dozens of actors and our chat was gossipy and full of reminiscences. After lunch we had a stroll through the markets; it is very much a town I would like to return to and get to know.

Monday 8 May
Back in Paris by 15.30. I got stuck, electronically, in the luggage section of our carriage for over five minutes. The train emptied and no amount of shouting and thumping could attract the attention of M and Marriott, who stood on the platform vaguely looking for non-existent porters. Finally I was

released, manually, by a stray passenger who had re-entered the train to collect a paper bag.

Paris seems cheerful. Everyone we have spoken to expresses delight at Chirac being president. Jacques Tual, an old friend, who dined with us at L'Orangerie, and who I have always assumed to be mildly left-wing, was emphatic in his admiration for Chirac, saying he has done a lot for Paris in the past fifteen years and now might do the same for France.

At the next table sat a handsome, middle-aged Hollywood type whom I couldn't place. He was wearing the smartest navy blue suit I have seen since that worn by Khrushchev's personal photographer, whom I met twenty-five years ago. Tailored by Lanvin I should think. His initials were embroidered on the top of the cuffs of his cream shirt but were too discreet for me to read. The shoulder padding a bit much—I imagine not to the taste of the tailor.

Tomorrow we Chunnel our way home.

Thursday 18 May
Yesterday to St Thomas's Hospital to see Bobby Flemyng. The situation looked the same as a month ago: no speech or movement (except slightly in the left hand) but a brightness in his eye.

In the evening Tom Courtenay and I dined at Interlude de Chavot in Charlotte Street. At next table sat two young men and two girls. We

31

felt they didn't know each other very well. One of the men asked the other if he wore jewellery, which seemed very unlikely. They all shrieked, puffed airily on their cigarettes and then reverted to talking of stocks and shares. They were a world away from Tom with his enthusiasm for soccer, the flute, Mozart, stargazing and, most recently, climbing plants. I am always amazed at how swiftly he becomes knowledgeable about whatever he takes up.

Today I took a dislike to the wrist-watch I foolishly bought recently. The strap is irritating and the second and minute hands are identical. I shall give it away. I want a watch I need only glance at to see the time and not have to peer at it. So this afternoon I went to Asprey's to look for what I wanted. Found it; at double the price I expected to pay. The likeable young man who sold it me shook my hand in a congratulatory way, as if he had presented me with a prize. First Prize for Extravagance.

Went to see Alfred Wallis exhibition at Crane Kalman Gallery. Much that I coveted but I couldn't afford half a picture, even if I hadn't bought the watch.

In the post a suspicious-looking packet which I opened cautiously. It turned out to contain three CDs from Tom, of Horszowski playing Beethoven, Chopin and Debussy. Horszowski is T's latest up-to-the-minute enthusiasm.

Monday 22 May
Bobby died in the early hours.

Much of the day I have busied myself making notes on the small parts in Shakespeare, often nameless, which are rewarding to the actor if only he'll not dismiss them as beneath his dignity. If I can work it up into a talk I might call it, 'Only a cough and a spit'—the phrase so often used by actors to explain away a lack of opportunity.

'Charles's Wain is over the new chimney,' and 'The star is fallen. Time is at his period,'— well worth saying, but from nameless characters. And dozens more.

The tadpoles in the pond are plumping up. The koi carp and blue orfe are looking lively and sleek. Life is very insistent; and it always seems to be so when friends sadly leave us.

Friday 26 May
Almost daily we read of the outside interests of Members of Parliament—declared or undeclared. Today I was reminded of going to the House of Commons in 1950 to seek information about the etiquette of points of order (such as putting on a hat) in mid-Victorian times. I was about to play Disraeli in a film (*The Mudlark*) and wished to bone up on my part. I asked Benn Levy, an MP and friend, if he could help. He said, 'Come with me and we'll ask the Father of the House [Winterton].

He is sure to know.' Winterton, when found, stooped from his immense height to listen to my query. Then he asked, 'For which company are you making the film?' I told him it was for 20th Century-Fox. 'I have an interest in the Rank Organization,' he said, 'and I couldn't possibly give information to a rival company.' With that he cranked himself upright again and stalked away, his interest very much declared.

Wednesday 31 May
What I would really like to see in the Former Yugoslavia (this has become too much of a mouthful) would be for some British corporal to get hold of Karadžić by his bouncing hairdo and give him a short-back-and-sides. Then release him. I am confident it would reduce his TV appearances and, who knows, hasten peace. And lower my blood pressure.

Wednesday 7 June
Took delivery this morning of a splendid new Wheel-Horse motor mower called Toro. It seems capable of doing almost everything except cook dinner. It looks lovely at the moment but I see an alarming glint in our lady gardener's eye—I think she is imagining herself winning at Le Mans or Monaco.

It seems a pity that the good old phrase 'living in sin' is likely to be dropped by the C of E. So many friends, happily living in sin, will feel very ordinary and humdrum when they become merely partners; or, as the Americans say, 'an item'. Living in sin has always sounded daring and exotic; something to do, perhaps, with Elinor Glyn and her tiger skin.

Sunday 11 June
I don't believe it is just that bosses in the armed services should be permitted to ask anyone if he is homosexual. What is more, it is almost as absurd as if they were to say, 'Are you now, or have you ever been, a shoe fetishist?'

During the 1939–45 hostilities I was impressed by an officer who, I surmised, was possibly attracted to his own sex. The only indication was his almost parental concern for the welfare of the men under his command. No bad thing.

Tuesday 13 June

Last night watched TV programme (put together by Terry Pratchett) on orang-utans in Borneo. It contained a remarkable few minutes of a huge male orang-utan, which had a face like a flat oriental mask, walking—red hair rippling—with a deliberate, undulating, unstoppable movement towards the camera. Then it sat down and contemplated us. I shouldn't have used the words 'which' or 'it', but 'who' and 'he'. He was a God of the Rain Forest with a mesmeric personality. It was the most impressive thing I've seen on the box this year; always excepting Miriam Rothschild's half-hour in March.

Must have my eyes tested. Today I found myself making enticing cooing sounds to what I took to be a rather pale pigeon on the lawn outside my study. It turned out to be a knuckle-bone left by one of the dogs.

Wednesday 14 June

Last night we went to Chichester to see *Hobson's Choice*. Enjoyable. The play stands up still, in spite of its overworking by repertory companies. Lovely acting from Nichola McAuliffe, Leo McKern and Graham Turner. Margaretta Scott's diction puts all to shame.

The all-too-close noise of traffic from the new A3 vibrates around the house; and yet when I stand by the pond I feel that the fish, slowly swimming up and down, create a deep silence which even the songs of blackbird and thrush hardly penetrate. But the weather makes it too cold to linger.

Friday 23 June
Yesterday afternoon I went to the British Museum hoping to look at a 4000 BC Egyptian ivory figurine of a lady wearing, apparently, a pair of huge dark glasses of lapis lazuli and nothing else. I had seen a picture of her and guessed she would do well on the cover of *Vogue*. Milling, scampering children were too exhausting on a hot day so I abandoned my quest and settled for half a dozen p.c.s of the lady. She looks a little hunched and chilly; now that I've got her picture home I notice she has only got seven toes in all.

Bumped into Dirk Bogarde in Fry's splendid vegetable shop in Cale Street. He was fingering oddly shaped tomatoes with a knowledgeable air. He rejected them and cast a dark eye over some frivolous greenery. He finally settled for a big, shiny, yellow pepper. I was envious of his concentrated marketing skill.

The media seem to have gathered round the national parish pump to discuss the challenge to the Prime Minister and Mr Hurd's resignation, and to speculate on Messrs Portillo, Lamont and Redwood. Barely a word about Sarajevo.

37

Friday 30 June

It is 90° around the house. (I can still only think in terms of Fahrenheit, yards, pints and ounces.) We opened all doors and windows to get a bit of air. Then I had the wheeze of changing into a nightshirt, pretending I was in the tropics, and all was fairly comfortable. The afternoon postman didn't turn a hair.

The 'scurvy politicians' are still at it; smiling at the cameras but clearly holding something sharp behind their backs. Their answers to questions are, as usual, blatantly evasive. Do they imagine we simple folk don't notice such things? When one of them threatened that a vote for so-and-so could mean the end of the Conservative Party for a thousand years I can't think why he imagined we should all throw up our hands in shocked horror. I imagine 50 per cent of the population wouldn't care a rap.

JULY 1995

Thursday 6 July
To Lewes by car. Held up for forty minutes by roadworks on A27 at back of Brighton. Nothing to relieve the boredom—not even a single Builder's Cleavage in sight; last year there were many rosy blossoms to be glimpsed at roadsides, on scaffoldings or quivering alongside pneumatic drills.

At Lewes I visited Keith Grant to look at some of his paintings. Bought one of a Norwegian fjord; very cool, calm and relaxing but with some turbulent brown and white clouds scudding across the mountains. He is a dab hand with rich blues.

On to lunch six miles away with John and Teresa Wells at their lovely manor house. Enviable position, enviable gardens. Blissfully quiet.

Spent the evening reading Patrick O'Brian's *HMS Surprise*. The smell of the sea lifts off his pages together with that of tar and the oiliness of so many Mediterranean harbours. His description of a storm in the south Atlantic catches one's breath away with fear and excitement. This is the third of his books I have read (in the wrong order) and I am now resolved to climb up the rigging of all of them.

Friday 14 July
'This *is* Bastille Day!' a young lady assured us on BBC Radio 4 just before the eight o'clock news this morning. She didn't sound the least bit French and I am sure no one had contradicted her.

On Wednesday went to see my doctor who said my blood pressure is lovely. Surprising. He said nothing about me being overweight but I caught a look in his eye and pleaded pressure of business and escaped before he could wag a finger. So, on to a lovely, large and entertaining luncheon party. But it was too hot. Sat, very grandly, at same table as Duchess of Gloucester. A rotund lordship lowered himself beside her. 'Well, young lady,' he said, 'tell me who you are. What's yer name?' HRH gave him the details with simple charm and not a trace of offence. He was silent for a while.

Friday 21 July
Watched BBC2 Proms Concert. Mahler's 8th Symphony. Thought the singing admirable but there were horrors of translatese in the subtitling; I would have preferred to have been left in blissful ignorance. Somewhere at the top of the seemingly endless tiers of choristers—a sort of singing Tower of Babel—was a venerable gentleman who looked like Charles Darwin. The cameras only gave one glimpse of

him; I longed to know what he was thinking. He looked concentrated and yet far away, as if saying to himself, 'So *these* are the fittest to have survived.'

An awful lot of cant is being said and written about the Lottery. Surely, before any thought of benefits to charities, etc., the average healthy punter has a silly hope of being a multimillionaire overnight. *Then* he would have the pleasure of selecting his own charitable donations.

Tuesday 25 July
Did a little two-minute talk about John Mills for Channel 4. To be shown next January, I think. An agreeable task. Pamela Hartwell always referred to him, affectionately, as 'Mr England'—and that just about says it all—the integrity, the kindliness, the determination, the good humour and strong sense of duty.

In the evening dined with Faith Brook, recently back from playing Volumnia (in *Coriolanus*) up north. The plaudits of the Tribunes and Citizens of Leeds are still ringing in her ears, I hope. I'm very fond of her but I fear she is sharpening the scythes on her chariot wheels to mow down politically incorrect rubbish such as myself.

Friday 28 July
A distinguished, well-written and amusing TV film script arrived this morning. A very small

part, so far as I'm concerned, but that is a relief these days. I intend saying 'Yes' on Monday but the sadness is that the dates of filming clash with an invitation to a holiday in a villa on Lake Como which M and I were looking forward to. The film will take me to Cambridge for a short while. Oh, dear! I want my Cambridge cake and to eat it on Como.

A vast balloon hummed its way towards the house as we were finishing dinner. It looked as if it was going to land in an adjacent field. The dogs went wild with excitement, leaping in the air as if to take a bite out of it, but the balloon slowly rose over a hedge, fancy free, and disappeared from sight. Dido, our border terrier, returned to us with triumph written all over her, well satisfied that she had seen off a giant and seeking our grateful praise. And a biscuit.

AUGUST 1995

Monday 7 August
Yesterday it was almost impossible to escape the Hiroshima and Nagasaki bombs of fifty years ago—eyewitness accounts, horrific photographs, speculations about political trickery and, of course, the insoluble moral dilemma. In some obscure way it seems ironical that the dropping of the first atomic bomb was on the Feast of the Transfiguration. 'A bright cloud overshadowed them.'

This evening I cleaned out our two plastic wasp-and-fly traps of the disgusting corpses floating in a mixture of honey, water and raspberry vinegar. To my horror it occurred to me that the traps looked like miniature mushroom clouds.

Played a CD of Beethoven piano sonatas to ease myself away from morbidity.

Wednesday 9 August
Mururoa. I have a sneaking admiration for the out-and-out obstinacy and flagrant selfishness of the French. 'I'm all right, Jacques.' It is such a surprisingly defiant attitude from the most civilized nation.

Today is the fiftieth anniversary of the bomb on Nagasaki; and somehow, perhaps because Nagasaki takes second place to Hiroshima, its

43

plight was the more distressing; maybe because it is known to have a large Christian population. Yet what difference should that make?

My left eye, which has been useless for ten years, has finally packed up. I see nothing with it except vast black octopus tentacles slowing crawling over a dark red background—and sometimes not even that. Tomorrow I go to consult my oculist.

Friday 11 August
'It will *possibly* clear in about six months,' he said. February seems a long way off. Apparently it is a flow of blood into the jelly of the eye. I feel I am ripe to play something in *King Lear*.

On Thursday evening to see Ayckbourn's *Communicating Doors*. The Feydeau-farce-like moments are very funny, the thriller bits reasonably chilling, but I did get somewhat confused by the time-warp story line. 'Once more into that suspect cupboard,' I thought, 'and I shall have to check up the time warp registered on my watch.'

It's odd that plays about time and its tricks—*Outward Bound, Berkeley Square*, the Priestley explorations of Dunne's theories—appeal and intrigue but don't finally add up.

When I got home this evening thistledown was streaming from the south-east over the

parched land like tens of thousands of
Chinook 'copters.

Sunday 27 August
Jill Balcon, Keith Baxter, Alan Bennett, M and
I lunched, in a very casual way, under the
tangled strawberry vine and spreading fig tree
(with its wooden fruit) in what I refer to as the
kitchen arbour. We felt quite jolly in the
dappled sunlight and could easily persuade
ourselves we were five hundred miles farther
south. I went into the kitchen to make coffee
and while I was there a fan and her female
friend worked their way through the hedge
with a gift (God knows what) for me. She
didn't spot me. M said I wasn't available and
asked her to leave. Luckily the dogs didn't
attack, which would have left me open to legal
proceedings, I suppose, for occupying my own
land and protecting my privacy. The lady has
been a nuisance for many years, sending me
unwanted pyjamas, for instance, at Christmas.
I have never met her.

Fans can be very dangerous; the history
of theatre, films and the music world is
littered with corpses stabbed or shot by
enthusiasts. And I wonder how many innocent
performers have been ruined by vengeful
blackmailers.

Before the war I was pursued to a number of
provincial theatres by a large, blonde girl. I
spoke to her only once, at a stage door, begging

45

her to cease spending money on me. I think she must have been a sweetly deranged office worker. Her gifts varied from bath salts to writing cases in bright blue imitation crocodile skin; things she greatly fancied for herself I expect. I knew her name and dreaded it. Then one day, in a provincial paper, the name cropped up again. The poor thing had been arrested for shoplifting in Boots the Chemists. I fear I had been the unsuspecting receiver of stolen goods. I'm glad she hadn't spent her own money on them.

But perhaps by the time of her arrest she was pouring out her cornucopia of Boots products at other and more appreciative feet. I do hope the magistrate dealt kindly with her.

Wednesday 30 August
Yesterday morning there was a read-through of Jack Rosenthal's TV play (temporary title, 'Interview Day') at the Irish Club in Camden Town. It is a complicated building for which Ariadne ought to supply a thread to get to the inner sanctum and out again. The reading went swimmingly well, I thought. In the afternoon Piers Haggard rehearsed James Fleet, who plays my son, and me in our brief scenes. Piers very on the ball but I cannot see in him anything of his father, Stephen, who died in the 39/45 war, whom I knew fairly well and was enchanted by as an actor. He taught me how to play backgammon. I think the TV will be a

happy assignment. But, oh, my failing memory.

This morning I wasn't wanted so took myself to the Sainsbury wing of the National Gallery to see the 'Fighting Temeraire' exhibition. It is an eye-opener to a great painting, wonderfully revealing the old order giving way to the new, and the new of the mid nineteenth century, as we know, already lost in the past. The sharply silhouetted black sails of Turner's 'Burial at Sea' conjure up a sad nightmare; his way with black smoke is somehow appalling, acrid and choking.

Lunch to Freda Berkeley, and then we went scrounging for kitchen oddities at Divertimenti in Fulham Road. I came away with a wire meat cover, looking like a fencing mask, and Freda with white truffle oil and some whizzing contraption.

SEPTEMBER 1995

Friday 1 September
Slept badly, my mind ruminating on Tuesday's rehearsal. What seemed OK at the time I now feel lacked simplicity. It doesn't get immortalized on film until Monday week—time enough for me to get into my usual panic. Must resist telephoning Piers about my anxieties.
Anyway I know my lines and can get through them while shaving.

Saturday 2 September
A clap of thunder and then welcome rain for half an hour. Proper rain, not the feeble drizzle we've had a couple of times in the last few days; but I fear it hasn't come in time to save parched trees, which look autumnal and rattle their brittle leaves.
Thinking back on Piers Haggard's father, Stephen, I remember he wrote a book with the doom-laden title of 'I'll Go to Bed at Noon'—a quote from Lear's Fool. He wrote it not long before he tragically died. I, also, want to use one of the Fool's lines as a title for something—'Winter's not gone yet, if the wild geese fly that way.' Can't think how to shorten it.
Is there any connection between wild geese

49

and Lady Wildgoose? Lady W and her sister Lady Sandys tried, in 1603, to get their old father Brian Annesley registered as insane. They were frustrated by their sister Cordell. Shakespeare must have heard gossip about it.

The teaching of games: Stephen Haggard taught me how to play backgammon, Michael Gough taught me to play mah jong, David Niven introduced me to croquet (on a very sporting course at his Hollywood home) and my mother instructed me in whist and rummy when I was about ten. But I still fumble my cards.

Monday 4 September
Merula, in an inexplicable ethnic mood, bought a loaf of bread which advertised itself as 'Made from an old Spanish receipt'. It was unbelievably disgusting. After attempting to eat half a slice we chucked the whole thing out to the old crow who visits us twice a day. He was thrilled and gouged out the nuts and green bits before you could say Juan Robinson.

Finished Trollope's *The American Senator*. The opening chapters are a bit wearily confusing but once he has got thoroughly underway it is enthralling. Arabella Trefoil is a great creation and for sheer awfulness matches Sylvia Tietjens in Ford Madox Ford's *Parade's End*. I've come across her several times, in various disguises but always recognizable, in London, Paris, Cairo and New York—but she lives mostly in Sussex.

I want to read the Peter Ackroyd biography of Blake but before that I think I'll go back to Patrick O'Brian's *The Wine-dark Sea*. How well O'Brian is served by the jacket illustrations of Geoff Hunt.

Making inquiries about Reid's Hotel in Madeira for a short holiday in October. I need Atlantic air but I'm not sure I like the idea of dressing up for dinner. Collar and tie, yes, but not patent leather shoes.

Friday 8 September
The invention of all weapons of indiscriminate destruction from the crossbow to the Doodlebug and the atom bomb is to be deplored; but atomic energy is undoubtedly here to stay and I would rather the French and ourselves had efficient atomic weapons than any other nation. I certainly don't like the idea of us being toy boys for the Presidents of Russia or the USA—or their wives. The French have proved they don't pussy-foot when it comes to dangerous issues and I, for one, shall continue to buy their wine and cheese and dream of French holidays.

Photos of the Tahitians destroying their own capital city in the name of non-proliferation of violence are nauseating. Is Greenpeace partially responsible for this idiocy? Greenpeace seemed so brave and glamorous when it first got going, bouncing over the sea in rubber dinghies to give hope to whales. Now, I fear, its activities are over-inflated.

Thursday 14 September
Started TV film last Monday. I fluffed or dried up a few times; shaming, as I have very little to say. Years ago if I fluffed on film it was usually an instinctive disapproval of some line I was required to say. That doesn't apply at all in this case. I shall put it down to finding eight in the morning to seven fifteen in the evening, in rather airless conditions, too long a day for someone shortly to knock up eighty-two years. That's going to be my excuse, anyway.

It is a very agreeable, good-humoured unit and James Fleet is a pleasure to act with. The location was the interior of a pretty, pink-washed house, totally tucked away in a quiet corner of Clapham. It is so hidden I doubt if the postman finds it with ease; just the sort of London house I'd love to own; blissfully quiet except for aircraft wandering to Heathrow and the owner's sweet-natured, snuffly pug-dog.

Back to the Connaught pretty tired and dined alone. At the next table sat two smart American women and their husbands. They were discussing female circumcision in some detail. 'I don't go for it,' said one of the women. I regretted having ordered an entrecôte and buried myself in Paul Vaughan's *Exciting Times in the Accounts Department*—very entertaining.

Sunday 17 September

The guttering around the roof has been splashing rainwater all over the place for three days and the grass has reappeared, a brighter green than is usual at this time of year. Went up to London yesterday and dined with Piers Paul Read and his wife; always pleasant and interesting company.

This afternoon I was driven to Cambridge and am spending a couple of nights at Forte's Posthouse Hotel, which advertises itself as giving 'The Warmest Welcome in Britain'. Well, maybe; but not on a damp Sunday afternoon.

The TV set in my bedroom kept announcing, in an admonitory way (rather like Kitchener's finger pointing 'Your Country Needs You!') 'There is a Message for You.' I switched channels and there it was again. Finally I managed, after five minutes' button-hopping, to get the message; from my agent as it turned out. I assume it wasn't shown on everyone's screen. It took another few minutes to find out—well, by chance, really—how to turn the bloody thing off.

James Fleet, Anna Carteret, Tom Wilkinson and I had a meal together. Much of what was on the menu was 'sizzling' or 'jumbo'. Wilkinson and I sampled the fish-'n'-chips; the others tackled more exotic dishes. The ice-cream was rather jolly. What on earth did we

53

talk about? Anna Carteret kept us spellbound and open-mouthed with her appalling account of being falsely accused of shoplifting; I bored everyone, until their eyes were thoroughly glazed, by endlessly and inadvertently name dropping. Garbo, Dietrich, Diana Cooper, *et al.* Oh, but I realize now, with some relief, that I never mentioned Chaplin, Grace Kelly, Ernest Hemingway or the Queen Mother.

Monday 18 September
I think the TV unit has finished with me; so long as nothing disruptive to the film is done in the labs. It was a pleasant little job but it came home to me, almost savagely, that age has withered memory, alertness has taken a tumble and custom staled what talent was there. More so than I had reckoned.

A smiling, pleasant chap, probably in his thirties, accosted me near the station with, 'Could I have your autograph?' He proffered paper and biro. I was graciousness itself and wrote, 'Good wishes' followed by my name. 'Thanks ever so,' he said. 'My granny will be thrilled.'

Tuesday 19 September
Left Cambridge by car at 09.30 in a mist. An hour later, over the car telephone, came the message that yesterday's filming was in the clear. As soon as I arrived in London I shaved off the ragged moustache I've been sprouting

for the past five weeks and after that visited Trumper's to have my remaining white hairs trimmed to respectability.

Spent a happy easy-going evening with Alan B, each of us shouting indiscretions over the muzak in Bruno's. He once described John Gielgud as having an iron streak running through him, of tinsel. I hope I'll laugh at whatever similar summing up he may make of me.

Tomorrow home; beloved wife, dear dogs, intelligent cat, outrageous rabbits, Himalayan molehills and the tumult of country noises.

Monday 25 September
During the last few days the media have treated us to accounts of statues of the Hindu god Ganesha 'miraculously' drinking pints of milk in temples from Southall to New Delhi. I don't give more credence to this phenomenon than I do to plaster Madonnas shedding tears of blood but I long to know what it is in the human make-up which relishes such apparently meaningless happenings. We are told that capillary attraction is a possible scientific explanation for Ganesha's addiction to the milk bottle, so I put a teaspoonful of water to the mouth of a stone figure of a Chinese courtesan we possess. She didn't take a sip but dribbled it all down her front.

In February 1984, when filming the deadly *A Passage to India*, Peggy Ashcroft and I escaped from Bangalore for a day to visit the ancient Hindu temple of Srirangapatan, not far from Mysore. I can't remember if Ganesha was represented there (his elephant face is always arresting and attractive) but there were dozens of set pieces, like small scenes in an end-of-pier Fun Show, of various glittering deities. The only one that three or four people—Indians in European clothes—were paying homage to, by turning round three times in front of her image, was Laksmi, goddess of wealth and luck. Her ropes of jewellery looked a bit suspect to me— but then no one was offering her milk or anything else. Perhaps she would do better on the empty plinth in Trafalgar Square with Lottery hopefuls, such as myself, gyrating before her. Or she could be placed so she could beam her smile at No. 11 Downing Street.

Thursday 28 September
Merula and I arrived at the Grand Hotel, Eastbourne, yesterday lunchtime. A warm welcome. It was a beautiful day; the sky powder-blue with a few Constable clouds, the sea a chalky green. It was good to glimpse again, before we reached Beachy Head, the River Cuckmere winding its narrow way in extravagant loops down to the sea. There were a few canoeists about but hardly any holiday-makers. It used to be an enjoyable picnic spot.

Eastbourne looks prosperous and clean. It has expanded vastly, particularly to the east, since I was last here about forty years ago. I was at school here from the age of fourteen to eighteen. There are new, ugly, dark red brick estates in the Crumbles area but the marina is impressive. Fairly early in the century there was a horrendous murder at the Crumbles which was still often referred to in the dormitories after 'lights-out' even in my day. As far as I can recall it concerned a man who chopped up his wife in little bits to make soup. It was a murder that appalled the nation for a decade. Nowadays such horrors are almost weekly events and cause little more than a brief pained frown.

Bobby's, the outfitters, just off Terminus Road has given way to Debenham's. On the first floor of Bobby's there used to be a splendid tearoom, complete with a few potted palms, where occasional treats were given to their offspring by visiting parents. Cream buns with raspberry jam and chocolate éclairs were politely but swiftly demolished while a sad trio scraped out 'In a Monastery Garden', 'Humoresque' or 'The Dance of the Hours'. The younger ladies wore cloche hats and some of the elderly spotted veils; hats were even more essential than gloves.

The pier theatre burned down twenty years ago but I well remember two productions, both appalling, which I saw there in 1930 and 1931. The first was Ben Greet's very lazy offering of *Julius Caesar*, in which it was obvious that most of the men had spent the day sunbathing on the beach; they were scarlet except for white areas, revealed by togas or Roman armour, where their one-piece bathing costumes with shoulder straps had protected them. Ben Greet himself shuffled around as Casca and you caught glimpses of his rolled-up trousers under his costume.

The other production was *The Merchant of Venice* with the old (as it seemed to me) actor-manager Henry Baynton as Shylock. He looked remarkably like the photographs of Irving in the part. I was rather impressed. He made very sinuous gestures with his right arm by way of greeting and these I practised (and got to perfection) in the cricket pavilion through most of a summer term. I had no interest in cricket. Baynton, sadly, was a lush. It was at Worthing, I think, and not at Eastbourne, that he presented his *Macbeth*. On a memorable night of high winds, crashing waves and lashing rain he decided there was time for him to battle his way to the nearest pub while Malcolm and Macduff set about their long tedious scene together, which was followed by Lady M prowling about in her sleep. No Macbeth appeared when Lady M left the stage washing her hands. After a considerable pause the lady stage-manager stepped before the curtain and announced to the bewildered audience—mostly schoolchildren who were studying the play for exams—'You can go home now. That is where the play ends.' So they left, raincoated and capped, doubled up against the elements. Imagine their fright when they saw, blown towards them, the figure of Macbeth in Viking helmet and cross-gartering, black wig flying and beard awry. In a rather hurt actor-laddie voice he called out to them. 'What? Going home so soon?' He staggered on his lonely way.

I never met him, but some years later, playing at the Savoy Theatre, a note was delivered to me just before a performance. It read, 'My name will mean nothing to you but I wonder if you would oblige a fellow Thespian with the loan of a fiver? I have to be in Liverpool tomorrow morning for a rehearsal and I have lost my railway ticket. I have no money. Henry Baynton.' I sent up the fiver. Also, by chance, I happened to know he was supposed to be in a play rehearsing in Liverpool. A day or two later I made inquiries. He had never turned up. I wish I had made it a tenner.

Friday 29 September
Eastbourne continued. The Devonshire Park Theatre is where I saw, in my early teens, most of the plays that came there in the holidays. I suppose it was where my enthusiasm for theatre was first nourished. Each week a new show arrived 'Straight from the West End' or 'Prior to London'. Stars such as Godfrey

Tearle, Owen Nares, Irene Vanbrugh and Phyllis Neilson-Terry alighted frequently— sometimes in frothy comedies, or thrillers, and now and then in what were considered torrid sex dramas. They were all welcomed by me. Most plays seemed to take place in the hall of a great country house or on the terrace of a smart hotel where there was a ball in Act II. The characters in the programmes nearly all bore titles but of course there were comic maids and cheeky footmen to put you in the picture. (Come to think of it that is more or less the device Chekhov uses in the opening of *The Cherry Orchard*.)

The Student Prince and his drinking chums thumped their steins of Bavarian beer; they were followed by *The Maid of the Mountains* and something very sloppy called *Wild Violets*. Also Sir Frank Benson brought his Shakespearean company—all able cricketers. They gave us *The Tempest* and *A Midsummer Night's Dream*. Benson (in his seventies) made a very thin Caliban, dressed in a sort of romper suit of hairy ginger material in which he swung about, rather cautiously, on a rope. In the *Dream* he played the not very taxing part of Theseus in a sleepy sort of way. At about this time I started taking *The Stage*, in which was the famous advertisement inserted by Benson, 'Wanted urgently; a Lorenzo who can keep wicket.' That sounded dismaying to me but I learned, from the same paper, that actors could earn as much as £12 a week. 'An actor's life for me,' I thought, 'cricket or no cricket.' But I never applied to Benson for a job.

I hoped while we were in Eastbourne to find the little secondhand bookshop where so much of my pocket money had been spent on Robert Louis Stevenson (Tusitala Edition), Ruskin, Ella Wheeler Wilcox (for the absurdity of it), John Masefield, Granville-Barker, Chesterton and H. G. Wells. Boutiques have crowded it out. And the public library was bombed during the war.

Somewhere in the town, but I can't remember where, I had bought my first stick of greasepaint—Leichner's No. 2½, a shocking pink. I smeared it all over my face, painted in thick black eyebrows (*à la* George Robey) and went to a local fancy-dress thé dansant.

During one Christmas holiday in London I was taken to a fancy dress ball at the Town Hall in Kensington and I went as a candle and candlestick. I was sixteen. I fashioned a white tubular arrangement out of cardboard to go on my head, and from crêpe paper a yellow and blue candle-flame; also a wide white cardboard collar. I won the first prize, which was a large, brown, fibre suitcase. But it was a humiliating experience as so many people flicked their cigarettes into my collar and then said, 'Sorry; thought you were an ashtray.' My fibre suitcase was small compensation.

Merula and I visited the theatre and it is

61

much as I remembered it; a bit smaller than Wyndham's I should think, but in the same style. It used to be pink and gilt; now it is mostly red and biscuit coloured. Very well kept. The packed audience consisted for the most part of elderly TV aficionados who nudged, wriggled and cackled at the dirtier jokes. It would have been a pleasure to have taken one or two of them out to the Crumbles. The title of the play? Ah, the name escapes me.

OCTOBER 1995

Sunday 1 October
A warm sunny day. Sam Beazley, whom I first knew in Gielgud's definitive 1934 production of *Hamlet*, is here for the weekend. I have only seen him two or three times in recent years. He gave up the theatre to run his very successful shop, Portmeirion, in Pont Street but during the past ten years or so has returned to acting. He also does admirable architectural sketches and spent a lot of time drawing, very accurately, our living-room.

He speaks Italian, pretty well, I imagine, and he gave us a riotous account of sharing a railway carriage with an Italian family. Apparently they started by talking about their relatives; then moved on to culinary information as they unwrapped their lunches; then discussed public scandals, about which they got very worked up. Finally it dawned on them that Sam was probably English and they bombarded him with questions about the Principessa Diana. The Principessa Di was too glorious for words, they thought, and they all wore happy smiles for the rest of the journey.

Tuesday 3 October
Last night the baby deer which has been enchanting us and our neighbours was killed.

Gunshots, far too close, were heard shortly after dark but we think it was killed by a fox. Its mangled body was found this morning a hundred yards from the house. Perhaps it was wounded by shot and finished off by a fox. The dogs sense everything. They were apprehensive last night and again this morning. They, I am sure, are guiltless. They have never chased deer; looking on them as goats and therefore sacred to my wife.

Thursday 5 October
To London. Lunched with Mu Richardson. Got myself an Oxford University pocket diary, which is the only thing that keeps me vaguely organized and which sensibly runs from October to October, thus enabling New Year to be spanned without fuss.

In the evening to the Theatre Royal, Haymarket, to see an American play called *Burning Blue*. Rather good and very well done. It is set aboard a fictional US aircraft carrier and deals with tracking down the love that *insists*, these days, on speaking its name. But it wasn't shrill. All the actors were excellent, but I particularly liked Ian FitzGibbon, who has a light and quirky touch, and the two girls, Katherine Hogarth and Helene Kvae. Some of the evening was too noisy for my taste, but when the decibels rose high they at least drowned out the heavy breathing in the audience of butch, leather-jacketed middle-aged men.

Back at the hotel I tried to get out of a lift as Eric Ambler was trying to get in. We had exactly the same encounter about three weeks ago. What is Providence trying to tell us? We nattered together for five minutes, verbally comparing failing eyesight and creaking limbs, sharing resentment—or maybe envy—at mutual friends who have boldly gone ahead. We stumbled apart, Eric to his bed, no doubt to dream up a thrilling plot for his next novel and me to the bar to down a cold lager.

Monday 9 October
Yesterday was startling for its beauty and warmth. We lunched outside off a picnic table and found it too warm to be wearing cardigans. 'Off, off, you lendings!' Today promises to offer another Indian summer. Our old dog Bluebell, who a week ago I thought was on her very last legs, suddenly rallied with the sunshine. After barely eating for days she wolfed down six frankfurters and some slices of Mr Kipling's almond cake and fairly bounded about the place.

In the evening we watched the second instalment of Kevin Brownlow's admirable programme on the early days of cinema. This time it was on the Scandinavians—not many jokes. As it started just after nine o'clock it meant I had a good excuse not to get het up about *Pride and Prejudice*, with its interminable dancing and knowing looks.

Thursday 12 October
Lord Home of the Hirsel has died. I met him
only once, at a dinner party at which I was
placed next to his wife. Conversation was a bit
stiff and, in desperation, I asked her how she
mostly spent her day when at home in the
Border Country. 'Good heavens!' she
exclaimed. 'I do what every woman in the
British Isles does. I spend the morning making
sandwiches and then take them down to the
men in the butts.' Lord Home stretched his lips
at me in a thin smile. He undoubtedly had
patrician charm but he made me feel very ill
bred.

Yesterday I listened to Sir Edward Heath on
the radio and thought how excellent and
balanced he is. I never cared for his
premiership but now I feel he is the only
statesman we have. What is more, when seen
on TV, he doesn't smile ad nauseam as so many
of the others do. I don't want to be wooed; I
want to be truthfully informed in a
straightforward manner.

Many MPs seem to have been gulled, like
Malvolio in *Twelfth Night*. Maria's fake letter
reads in part, 'If thou entertainest my love, let it
appear in thy smiling; thy smiles become thee
well; therefore in my presence still smile.' I look
forward to the day when Hon. Members will
sport yellow stockings and cross-gartering.

Friday 13 October
M wasn't feeling well yesterday and I thought it unwise that she should come with me to the matinée of Dürrenmatt's *The Visit* at Chichester; so I invited our good friend and neighbour Diana Parker. Before the performance I decided it would be sensible (oh, the tiresomeness of age) to visit the gents. As I was opening the door a vigorous woman of about sixty pushed past saying, indignantly, 'Excuse *me*!' I followed her. She got halfway to the urinals, gave a little yelp and whimper and rushed out, bumping me in the process. No apology of course. 'Toilet Rage' perhaps.

The play was interesting. I was under the impression I had seen the Lunts in it years ago but I didn't recognize it. Went round to see Betty Bacall, who feels she has been unfairly mauled by the critics. She'd be fine if she would get rid of her red wig and wear her own beautiful hair.

Monday 16 October
Merula is eighty-one today. We came up to London yesterday afternoon. M obviously thought she was expected to send supplies to the troops in the Crimean War—all the shoes she brought, other than the flat things she was wearing, were left-footed. And we are here for five days.

Good grouse for dinner in the Connaught

Grill but they forgot to put bread in the bread sauce; so what was ladled from a silver boat was a thin, runny, flavourless gruel.

M went to see eye specialist this morning to discuss removal of a cataract in six months' time. Matthew and friend for dinner at Cecconi's.

Tuesday 17 October
To Bobby Flemyng's memorial service at St Paul's, Covent Garden; a vigorous and happy event. Beautiful singing of 'Oh, for the wings of a dove' by Master Anthony Way, who looked like a bright robin in a white frilly collar. All the singing was good and the choir sang a piece from Verdi's *Nabucco* very finely. Didn't quite catch the jokes in Alan Bates's address, but churches are notoriously bad to speak in and I am aware of increasing deafness. Perhaps readers at St Paul's should use the pulpit and not the chancel steps.

We gave lunch to Lauren Bacall and Keith Baxter at Neal's. Marvellous clam and prawn soup. We shouted desperately at each other over the general din but didn't attempt to rise until 15.45, which means, I hope, an enjoyable time, if an exhausting one, was had by all. Betty Bacall looked stunning as a sort of female Hamlet; black trousers, black chiffon Armani blouse, black coat and black black black glasses. *That* is what she should have worn in *The Visit* at Chichester—and her own hair, *not* a red wig.

In the evening to see *Carrington* at the Curzon. Enjoyed it. The film a touch bitty perhaps, and even-paced and slowish. It got a move on when it came to the obligatory bonking, all of which was taken at the same heaving canter. Somehow it wasn't very erotic. Jonathan Pryce gives a truly marvellous performance as Lytton Strachey—100 per cent convincing. Emma Thompson better than I've seen her but I was doubtful about her skill as a painter. The only totally believable painting I've seen done on the screen was by Anna Massey as Gwen John a few years ago. The sets and décor in *Carrington* I thought imaginative and v.g. The script has wit. Did Dora Carrington *reely* have a Croydonish accent? I know it is ubiquitous these days, and we shouldn't notice, but it does rather kill the period flavour. I think Trevor McDonald is going to have a rough time trying to put it right.

Wednesday 18 October
This morning, accompanied by M's sister Chattie, we were kindly shown round the Globe Theatre (still under construction) by Mrs Bladget. There is much to be done but it is already impressive. Considering what sniping and counter-sniping there must have been among so many Shakespeare academics it is amazing it has got off the ground at all. The

position, so close to the river and with St Paul's Cathedral in the background, is very striking. I just hope the poor actors, sweating it out under a summer sky, aren't deafened by megaphones on the tourist boats informing the world, 'That's Shakespeare's Globe, his "Wooden O", burned down during a performance of *Henry VIII* on 29 June 1613.' By the time the guide gets that out his boat will have chugged under the bridge and another will have taken its place with the same information. Overhead aircraft will be droning their way to Heathrow. Oh, I wish the actors good fortune but I wouldn't wish to be wearing their buskins or chopins and having to face such competition. It is the acoustics that will cause the headaches. I can't see any line being able to be said 'trippingly on the tongue' as Shakespeare requested.

I wonder if, in *A Winter's Tale*, a real bear was borrowed from the adjacent bear-baiting pit to chase Antigonus near the end of Act III: 'Exit, pursued by a bear'—every actor's favourite stage direction.

The theatre looks larger than expected. I can't help feeling that, whatever the experts say, the stage is about half a metre too high. Actors need to look down on a section of the audience in order to feel in control but I don't believe the groundlings should have to crick their necks. The beautiful Theatre Royal in Bath made the same mistake, in my opinion, when during refurbishment it raised its stage uncomfortably high.

One encouraging thing I learned from our tour of the Globe is that the plaster used around the walls is mixed with goat hair. Many of our grand old provincial theatres have horsehair under their gilded decoration and this (or so I was told years ago) gives exactly the right resonance to the human voice. Walk on to the stage of any of those big old theatres and you know at once that you are going to be heard with very little effort.

You can stand in the centre of the vast semicircular theatre at Epidaurus, which I did some twenty years ago, and speak a piece of Shakespeare in an almost conversational tone knowing your voice will carry to the distant heights of the back row. For all our technology we don't compare with the ancients. I can't remember the number of people Epidaurus could hold; I'll hazard a guess of twelve thousand—anyway, more than the National, Chichester and the Barbican combined.

Friday 20 October
Red Rum has died; we all shed a tear. He has been buried close to the winning-post at Aintree, which shows the same sort of imagination as the dipping of the great cranes in the Dockland area as Churchill's body passed on its way up the Thames.

We came home at lunchtime today to find

71

Bluebell in almost bouncing form. I doubt if it will continue for long, but she has hung on with loving determination in M's absence.

Last night to Wyndham's to see *Three Tall Women*. I am clueless as to what the play is about; Maggie Smith is superb. It is a wonderfully disciplined performance; she could so easily have indulged the audience with what was expected but she remained valiant for truth. Sitting next to me was a pale man who should have been in bed at home—or in hospital. He wheezed, spluttered, coughed and took regular swigs from a medicine bottle; he endlessly scraped his empty ice-cream carton with a wooden spatula, a particularly irritating sound.

Sunday 22 October
Sore throat and headache; the responsibility, I'm sure, of the occupant of row A in the royal circle, seat no. 4, on Thursday night.

Monday 23 October
One of the nice things about feeling rotten is having a good excuse to stay in bed tucked up with an entertaining book. The book in this case is Piers Paul Read's *A Patriot in Berlin*. (Thank you, occupant of seat no. 4 in row A of Wyndham's royal circle.) If symptoms persist for another day or so I have at my side Gore Vidal's *Palimpsest*, which is thick enough to see me through an illness rather than an

indisposition.

Today I was supposed to lunch with Melvyn Bragg at the Ivy. I don't think I have been to the Ivy since 1947, when Jack Priestley took me there to tell me how good Cedric Hardwicke was as Abel Drugger, in *The Alchemist*, which I was playing at the time.

Builders arrived this morning to start work removing a bath and substituting a walk-in shower. I knew it was going to be noisy but hadn't expected their electric saws would set the smoke alarms pinging.

The cherry tree outside the kitchen is flaming red and the choisya, which flowered early in the year, is again in full bloom—something it has never done before.

Wednesday 25 October

On Monday night the heavens fell; or, rather, Merula did, heavily, tripping on a paving-stone. She has broken her right hip and was in great pain, which she bore with her usual fortitude. At noon yesterday her doctor ordered an ambulance. We left the house at 12.30, drove the eighteen miles to Queen Alexandra Hospital at Portsmouth and by 13.35 she had been examined (by a beautiful, shy, lady doctor), had gone through all the usual medical routines and had an X-ray taken. I was tremendously impressed by the hospital staff, by their charm and speedy efficiency. She is being operated on as I write.

Matthew came down yesterday afternoon to spend the night and to visit her, pre op., this morning. He was a great comfort to me; I hadn't realized until a few hours ago how shaken I have been; fits of trembling and a feeling of being off balance.

The hospital has just telephoned to say all went well. *Deo gratias.*

Tuesday 31 October
The last few mornings have started with a lot of mist but the sun has appeared in a cloudless sky after an hour or two. I have stopped trembling. M seems to be getting on pretty well and has even used her Zimmer frame, slowly and cautiously. I suppose it will be several weeks before she can climb the stairs. Tomorrow it is hoped she will be moved to our local hospital.

Canada is to remain Canada we are told. Anyway for the present. I have only been to Canada twice; in 1953 for a wonderful canoeing and fishing holiday on the French river prior to the first season of the Stratford, Ontario, theatre; and in 1964 when touring a play about Dylan Thomas before it opened in New York. I had a few days in Quebec and thought it bleak. Everyone loves Montreal but I never made it.

Most evenings when M and I are alone we play a CD—usually classical music. Last night I realized I hadn't played anything, or even lit the fire, since she has been in hospital. So I promptly put on some Schubert and saw life in a rosier hue. Then I took up a volume of Percy's *Reliques*, dusty with neglect, and went happily to bed, followed by the three dogs— Japheth bounding up the stairs in macho mood, Dido tiptoeing with feminine elegance and poor old Bluebell taking a hesitant step at a time. Perhaps she was showing empathy with Merula's efforts with the Zimmer.

NOVEMBER 1995

Monday 6 November
An extraordinary photograph, taken by the Hubble space telescope, has appeared in the papers over the weekend. It shows wild columns of gas and dust six million million miles high giving birth, we are told, to new stars. Two current catch-phrases come to mind—'How do they *do* that?' and, 'I don't *believe* it!'

When sorrows come, they come not single spies,
But in battalions.

On Saturday evening Matthew was viciously struck on the back of his head. He was taken to hospital for X-ray; reports are OK.
Rabin has been assassinated in Tel Aviv.
A police horse has been stabbed in the head by a football hooligan.
There seems to be no end to the senseless wickedness done on this little planet in a minor solar system, and we puny mortals appear to be decreasing in importance so far as the universe is concerned. Faith, Hope and Charity are easy to pray for but I fear that in my case they are receding at the speed of light. For the moment anyway. The past few days have been worse than I am prepared to commit to paper.

Wednesday 8 November
I don't think I have ever seen so many frenetic gestures as those displayed last night by a handful of Booker Prize commentators. Some of the literary hairdos rivalled the grimaces taking place underneath them. The Canadian Mountie TV 'Going South' was delightfully restrained and amusing, as usual.

To start rereading Ford Madox Ford's *Parade's End* for the third time, which I did when the Booker offerings were over, was a genuine, reliable pleasure. The characters deepen and become more subtle with familiarity.

I have turned down a handsome offer to play a slap-up part in a film opposite Jack Lemmon, whom I admire. A number of reasons: (a) it would be unsuitable to push off to the USA for three months in the present circumstances; (b) I can't see myself as an old American farmer of the 'Howdy doo, Dad?' variety; (c) I doubt if I could memorize the lines—too many; and (d) I am weary of TV, cinema or theatrical fare set in Old People's Homes. Too near the bare knuckle.

Friday 10 November
'There are more things in heaven and earth, Horatio,' etc., etc., and they can stretch from Hampshire to the Aegean Sea.

This morning I thought Bluebell was really

on the way out. I telephoned our admirable, caring vet and also arranged for a grave to be dug in the shade of a clump of silver birch trees where Bluebell has spent hours of her life gazing at people passing along a footpath. The vet came at noon and he thought the horrid day could be postponed. Apparently her heart is quite strong and she doesn't seem to be in pain. She has received an injection and lapped up a saucer of tea with honey. She looks a little brighter.

Fifteen minutes before the vet arrived the telephone rang. It was a bad, crackling line but I could just make things out. The call was from an old friend, Jehane West, who lives on the island of Amorgos in the Cyclades. She said she was worried as she hadn't heard from me for quite some time. (I last wrote about three months ago.) She said she wanted to know four things: how was Merula? how was I? how was Matthew (whom she has never met)? and, finally, how was Bluebell? (She didn't ask after the other dogs, or Michaelmas the cat.) All four questions were very much to the point. Jehane should alter her way of life. She should move from Amorgos to Delphi and, sitting on a tripod stool in the sanctuary, announce herself as a latter-day Pythia.

Monday 13 November
Bluebell collapsed on Saturday night; her hind legs ceased to function. The vet came yesterday

morning; she was gently put to sleep and then given a lethal injection. We buried her in her basket. It was a melancholy day of mist and drizzle. Still, she had a happy fourteen years and was loved by all who knew her. Friends put a posy of autumnal flowers on her grave. A tear was shed.

Kind neighbours took me to their house for lunch.

Today is gloriously sunny, mild and colourful. It looks like mid-October rather than well into November. And Merula comes home in two days' time.

I am happy that the two minutes' silence of Armistice Day, at eleven o'clock on the eleventh day of the eleventh month, is being observed again by many people. Something went wrong with the nation when the date was shifted, for commercial reasons, to a Sunday. Let us hope that the full Cenotaph ceremony will be returned to the proper date and all activity comes to a stop for that brief spell of remembrance.

Sunday 19 November
Holy Communion was brought to the house this morning for M. There is always a special good feeling about this; a particular domestic blessing. I was scared the dogs would be unwelcoming with loud barks but they were absolutely quiet.

Yesterday evening Keith Baxter for dinner,

who bravely risked my attempt at an Irish stew. It was OK, but hadn't enough white pepper. Always difficult to know what to drink with it. Whisky, for preference, I think, but I didn't offer that as Keith was to drive home. So we settled for champagne throughout the evening and it worked admirably. Not what you could call Potato Famine fare.

Keith asked me what my reaction would be if offered Friar Laurence in a production of *Romeo* he is thinking of. I said, which is sadly true, that I'd be fearful of being able to learn so many lines; also that the long speech the Friar has at the end, when he tells the assembled cast and the audience all that they have witnessed in the past two hours, is very tedious. I have seen weary actors trying to look interested and astonished at all the revelations and failing desperately. However, after I had gone to bed I had one of my somewhat insane fancies.

In a half-awake state I saw Fr. L dressed correctly (for once) as a Franciscan, entering with his cowl pulled over his head. According to the lines it is first light, pre sun-up, and he is alone. He might appear as a rather sinister figure—Death perhaps, with a pruning knife instead of a scythe. He carries, of course, his osier basket of wild flowers and herbs. He starts with the rather pretty speech, in rhyming couplets, about the good and baleful properties of various flowers (and curiously enough, of stones) before he is joined by

Romeo. He doesn't see Romeo to begin with but, picking up a flower, says, 'Within the infant rind of this weak flower/Poison hath residence and medicine power.' The speech ends with the words, 'Full soon the canker death eats up that plant,' and Romeo says, 'Good morrow, father!' Laurence acknowledges this with a blessing, '*Benedicite.*' That is the moment, I think, when he should throw back his cowl and appear as the ordinary man he is. (I have written to Keith suggesting half a dozen actors who would be revealed satisfactorily, rather than me.) There is more to the part than I had realized.

In today's *Observer* is a large photograph of a youngish man wearing pyjamas and looking sleepy. No explanation. After some thought I realized it was a still of me in the film of Priestley's *Last Holiday.*

A few days ago, somewhere, there was an equally large photo from the dismaying *A Passage to India.* Again it was me, in Hindu garb, and underneath it said it was me as Aziz. Not at all. Aziz was played by the admirable, young, handsome Indian actor Victor Banerjee. It seems the only press photographs we can rely on are of the Princess of Wales in gym work-out clothes. Aziz, of course, is a Muslim.

Wednesday 22 November
To London yesterday for a day and a night. Matthew came down to hold the fort here.

Bank, a haircut, household shopping. Lunched alone at Wiltons, wolfing an excellent Sole Colbert.

In early evening to a friend's flat where I made my long overdue confession to a holy and illuminating priest. It was a memorable experience which gently sponged away all my recent irascibility, anxieties and spiritual turmoil. Perhaps kneeling at a dining-room table is more relaxing than the upright coffin of an elaborately carved confessional. It would be good to think that from now on I shall spread only sweetness, light and understanding; but I fear I know myself too well. The bad habits of a lifetime, when tackled head on, seem only to bend, not break.

Dined with Alan B. National Gallery talk and wonderment over the palace drama which has riven the nation—in my opinion into the knowing and observant quarter of the population on one side, and the moist-eyed lovers of popular entertainment on the other. It is a series that is likely to run and run.

Thursday 23 November
A grey day. I have been thinking about Friar Laurence; or rather, not about Fr. L in particular but more to do with the prescience Shakespeare shows in some of the plays. Is it deliberate, accidental or totally unconscious? Probably just the way his mind worked. In *Macbeth*, of course, it is deliberate. The first encounter with the witches contains an evil

prophecy; their appearance brings to the surface his vaulting ambition, which possibly he hasn't fully recognized until then.

In *Antony and Cleopatra*, at the beginning of the play, the Soothsayer tells Charmian's future by reading her hand. He says, 'You shall outlive the lady whom you serve.' Charmian's comment on that is, 'O excellent! I love long life better than figs.' At the end of the play the Clown brings Cleopatra a basket of figs in which are nestled the asps which will kill her, and a few minutes later will kill Charmian.

I like to think the same actor played the Soothsayer and the Clown. It would make a good double, as well as working on the audience's unconscious memory of figs and death.

Tuesday 28 November

To London to do a few lines post-synching on TV film 'Interview Day', now unaccountably titled 'Igloo Day'. The recording studio was somewhere west of Paddington in a rather desperate-looking area; there were a few clutches of pretty little Victorian houses squeezed between grim blocks of flats on a dreary, wide, dank road. I was appalled by what I saw of myself on the screen—very old, very ugly in a feeble way and grossly fat. How come, I don't know; I certainly don't eat a lot, but I have given up walks. Bad.

I got back from a visit to the Garrick Club in

time to breathe in hot air from the Tate Gallery annual do. Much risky body language from the 'experts'.

A letter to Earl of Egremont, at Petworth; 1832 perhaps.

My Lord,

I have the temeraire to inform your l'dship that I intend visiting Petworth Park once more. I would be obliged if your l'dship would have the goodness to order that a cow and her calf should be felled so that I may make an artistic arrangement with their dismembered limbs. I shall have these displayed in a glass box at the Academy and I feel the whole nation will applaud my far-seeing ingenuity.

I have the honour to be,
  Yr l'dship's ob'd servant,
   J. M. Turner

PS. I shall bring my own carboys of formaldehyde.

PPS. I prophecy that in the near future galleries will be built, at the cost of millions of pounds sterling donated by a grateful people, to house similar artistic objects.

PPPS. The vigour of this concept of mine will, undoubtedly, put paid to accusations made by foreigners that our beloved country is slipping into decadence.

I fear I may sleep badly. AG   JMT

DECEMBER 1995

Monday 4 December
A blackbird sang so vigorously in the morning mist, so close at hand, and so persistently that I was astonished I couldn't see him. He never changed his position; somewhere among the fallen withered grapes, I think. The mist remained all day, sometimes making a fine drizzle; apart from the blackbird the day was soundless. Not even the traffic on the A3 intruded. It was almost spooky.

An old friend, Valieri Stavredi, died in the early hours in a nursing home; no friend or relative with him. He was ninety and had been ill for a year. We first met in New York during the war; I had gone there with dozens of others to collect our ships—well, LCI (L)s (large craft for transporting infantry)—being built near Boston. At that time Val was working for the Ministry of Information: later he became a UN official. He was a source of wit and worldly wisdom; he was also a passionate concert-goer and opera buff as well as being well read in the classics and a good linguist; accomplishments with which I couldn't compete.

When Merula and I went to Japan for a fortnight's holiday Val was in Tokyo in his UN capacity. I cabled him to book a table (a small room, as it turned out) in the best restaurant in town for our first night. He asked to bring a Japanese friend in case there were language difficulties. (In fact he managed well, having spent six years there.) He cabled back saying it would be very expensive. I replied I didn't care. So on our first evening in Tokyo we went to a very tasteful, quiet place set among pine trees. Our room was entirely beige—beige mats on the floor, on which we sat, and sliding beige screens which rustled slightly as they were opened and closed. A pretty girl in a flowered kimono sat just behind my right shoulder and kept filling my cup with sake. I didn't notice how many times she did this, as we were all silently busy chasing with chopsticks a radish, carved to look like a rose, which we each had in our delicious colourless soup. The pretty girl, in desperation I suppose at our lack of conversation, finally hissed something to my Japanese guest.

'What did she say?' I asked.

Val gave me a steady look and said, 'She says she greatly admires our Winston Churchill.'

A little later she made another attempt.

'What now?' I asked.

Val supplied the answer. 'She hopes honourable eaters like Picasso.'

Obviously our conversation was expected to be on a high level.

It was a memorable meal in many ways. When eventually I asked for the bill two middle-aged women slid open a screen and

88

entering on their knees prostrated themselves as they pushed a ribbon of meaningless paper towards me. Meaningless? It worked out at about £200 a head. But for that, of course, we were each given a pretty little doggy bag of the scraps we hadn't eaten.

Two or three years later I asked Val to do a translation of Diderot's *Le Neveu de Rameau*, which he did excellently. I had recently seen Fresnay (my favourite actor) in the part in Paris and thought I would like to attempt playing it. Peter Brook showed some interest in directing it but all came to nothing. Anyway it's not a play—just a long monologue with a few brief interruptions from another character. I shall always remember the frisson Fresnay caused when he held up a silver coin as if it were the Host at Mass. The worship of money, the sourness of poverty, the total contempt, the intelligent irony all seemed to be present in his simple gesture and derisive eyes. I'd go a long way to see acting like that again.

I also put in Val's way the translation of a good French film script. Hollywood didn't like it and that, as so often, was that.

Wednesday 6 December
Button-punching from channel to channel last night I finally alighted on BBC 2 sometime after nine o'clock. We thought we were seeing things. And indeed we were. We were confronted by a row of bare bums, bent over

and chattering and singing through their anuses. O horribilis! O horribilis! Most horribilis! 'How do they *do* that?' With latex buttocks and human lips I suppose. Come back, Mary Whitehouse. All is forgiven.

But then there was Mike Atherton soldiering on bravely and enduringly and successfully in South Africa. What a relief.

Monday 11 December
It is thawing and nearly all the thin blanket of snow we have had for the past few days is disappearing fast. A deer is standing stock-still in the paddock looking rather bemused. Very few birds have turned up for the nuts and seeds thrown out for them.

An invitation this morning to go to St Petersburg in mid-February to hear a performance, in the little theatre in the Hermitage, of a work by Roald Dahl set to music from works by Sibelius. Would love to go but daren't accept; February is likely to be an irksome month (it always is) with M's cataract to be sliced away and a possible operation on my blind eye.

Sister-in-law Chattie came for the weekend to help out with cooking. She's a dab hand in the kitchen. The dear people (the McCutcheons) who run the Harrow Inn, a few hundred yards from us, sent up a vast, excellent steak and kidney pie. M never makes pastry so I hadn't seen one of those porcelain chimneys poking through the crust for many years. It looked to me remarkably like the chimneys you see sticking out of the half-buried troglodyte houses in Murcia, in southern Spain.

Reading Teresa Waugh's *The Gossips* with great pleasure. Witty, gripping and a bit scarifying.

A new cooker and fridge arrived last Friday morning; a couple of lively, husky chaps had them installed and working in an hour. They came from Power House (formerly Southern Electric) in Havant. Before going to the showroom at Havant I tried another big firm, just outside Chichester, but decided firmly against them. They wouldn't guarantee a day of delivery and said it might take two days to take away the old stove and fridge and instal the new, and they would need two teams to handle it all. So they didn't get my order, which was for nearly £2000. Presumably Power House is happy; I think I am, although the cooker appears to have as many mysterious controls as Concorde. As I write I know it is flashing little green lights in the kitchen when it should be doing simply nothing. Over-excitement, perhaps, at the prospect of me burning saucepans.

Beloved Japheth (whitish Labrador type) was sick all over the bedroom floor at 4 a.m. Well, that had to be cleared up and he watched me, wagging his tail with relief that I hadn't barked at him. He was so pleased that he decided he would spend the rest of the night on my bed; consequently I had difficulty getting to sleep again, being apprehensive he might give a repeat performance.

Yesterday evening we watched, enthralled, Peter Ustinov's solo performance televised at the Alexandra Theatre in Toronto. To begin with I thought he was going to have difficulty with his audience, which appeared to me to be mostly composed of staid industrialists and their wives; but I was wrong. They quickly warmed to him. His amusing anecdote about me preparing to play Hitler in a film is wildly over-elaborated and barely 60 per cent true, but he can do with it what he likes as far as I am concerned. I am a fan; particularly of his more serious work, for which critics haven't given him his due.

When Richard Burton gave his *Hamlet* in Toronto it wasn't at the Alexandra but at the vast O'Keefe Centre. The opening night coincided with a Big Fight—I can't remember who was thumping whom. There was electricity in the air; the theatre fairly crackled with an extraordinary sound, which turned out to be about 2000 of the male members of the audience glued to the fight on their transistor radios with their eyes politely turned towards the stage: their spouses had their heads turned away from Hamlet, their eyes fixed on Elizabeth Taylor, who was sitting among them, glittering in real emeralds and green glass beads.

Tuesday 12 December
Googie Withers, her husband John and daughter Joanna for tea; they are having a week at Forest Mere health farm, so no cakes and ale. They must be just about the warmest, closest, kindliest family in the world; they exude happiness. Shortly after the great bush fire in NSW a few years back, Googie wrote a long, vivid letter in which she told how their house, on the outskirts of Sydney, had been in imminent danger of being engulfed by flames. They were warned to fill up their car with what they might need and be ready to make a dash for safety. She said they filled the car, not with essentials but with the irreplaceable—old photograph albums and family snaps. Typical of her to get the priorities right. The house was spared.

Wednesday 13 December
To London. Melvyn Bragg gave me lunch at the Ivy; I was impressed to be at what was obviously one of the No. 1 tables. Melvyn took the deference shown him with modesty and charm.

After lunch I started on a frenzied couple of hours' Christmas shopping, followed by a haircut and acute indigestion: I should never have had the 'crispy duck salad'. But a couple of Asilone tablets did the trick—an almighty burp, which shook Jermyn Street, was followed by instant relief.

Passed a youth, dossed down for a cold night in a shop doorway, who called out to me cheerily, 'Hi, Grandad! Go put the kettle on and make us a cuppa tea.' It made me laugh so I turned back and gave him £1. I was rewarded with a delightful young smile. I muttered, half to myself, 'I bet you say that to all the old men who shuffle past.'

Michael and Henrietta Gough, Alan B and I to dinner at L'Odéon in Regent Street, which opened last week. Micky Gough, vastly bearded and moustachioed for his part in *Mother Courage* at the National, looked as if he might be advertising Kentucky Fried Chicken. He won't mind me saying that; I've known him well and lovingly since about 1936. The restaurant is big and already doing a roaring trade; it looks likely to be one of the 'in' places, judging from the familiar faces we saw. Food good but over-prettified.

Alan, as usual, bicycled away, braving the surges of Regent Street traffic. The Goughs and I finally found taxis near Fortnum & Mason, having waved away offers of transport from dubious-looking cowboys.

We were unaware of the horrors of rioting in Brixton.

Thursday 14 December

The Christmas shopping rush continues—I try not to be bumped into by tourist children or bash other people's plastic bags or have little rages at the dotty indecisions shown at so many counters. Oh, that fumbling search through tired purses for the smallest coin and then offering a 50p piece. With huge relief I gave it all up at noon and went to Mass at Farm Street. The Feast of St John of the Cross, a favourite saint.

In the winter of 1964, working on the film *The Fall of the Roman Empire* in Spain, Tony Quayle rented a marvellous sixteenth-century farmhouse a couple of miles outside Segovia and kindly invited me to share it. Half a mile down the little river, which flowed by the house, is a Carmelite monastery and adjoining it the rather tatty small church where St J of X is buried. I visited his tomb several times and the place where he had first been laid to rest. He must have been a tiny man; it seemed to me he could have been folded up quite comfortably in a cigar box.

It was at the beginning of the war, many years before I became a Catholic, that I became interested, in a totally uncomprehending way, in the Spanish mystics. St Teresa of Avila's autobiography—which must be one of the greatest given to the world—set me off, reading it nightly by the kitchen fire in a tiny cottage we rented for a few shillings a week. As Teresa was a penfriend with St J of X I wanted to delve into him as well. But he is tougher going and hasn't the endearing jokes that make St T of A almost fun. Among qualities they have in common is a breathtaking honesty.

He must have seen often what we saw that bitterly cold winter; snow six feet deep in places and icicles at least sixteen feet long hanging from the walls of the Alcázar, which faces towards the monastery from across the river. Perhaps extremes of climate are healthy for the spiritual life.

Lunch with Mu Richardson and Keith Baxter in the warmth of the Connaught Grill. I have given a final 'No' to the idea of playing Friar Laurence.

Saturday 16 December
Today I have felt querulous. Behaviour has been spiky; largely due, I think, to our affable postman dutifully pushing piles of junk mail through the letter-box daily. It gets worse near Christmas. The rubbish, the charity appeals (often in duplicate) and, worst of all, the photographs from *Star Wars* demanding autographs. They mostly come from America and as often as not enclose a stamped addressed envelope—the stamps being US stamps, are useless here. The English usually make their demand without photograph, envelope, stamp or money. The nation has got

acclimatized to asking something for nothing. Bills in the post are welcome in comparison. It's mean and hard of me but from 1 January 1996 I am resolved to throw it all in the waste bin unopened (bills excepted, of course); I no longer have the energy to assist teenagers in their idiotic, albeit lucrative, hobby.

It has been one of those days when you hit your thumb with a hammer or spill a bottle of milk. Also M and I had a severe argument about whether a rack of tiny lamb cutlets, weighing 2 lb, should take 20 or 40 minutes in the oven. Jill Balcon is coming to a meagre dinner so she can arbitrate between us or make her own decision. She is, after all, a Queen of the Kitchen and cooks at a high level in a high-level oven—always a sign of know-how. Our oven is only waist high.

This evening Rodney Bennett telephoned. I have worked with him twice (the last time on Graham Greene's *Monsignor Quixote*) and we get on chattily and easily. Some time ago I suggested he should direct a film or TV of J. M. Barrie's 'Farewell Miss Julie Logan'—a marvellous, pawky, touching ghost-like story. He was telephoning to say he has found the right writer and things look like moving ahead. He would do it beautifully so I keep fingers crossed that someone will back him to the hilt. If I win the Lottery I shall.

I see the lights of Jill's car coming up the drive. *Elle approche*; bearing, I know, a vast ham she has cooked, together with a variety of beans and parsley sauce. It is for tomorrow's lunch, when we shall have 'the beauty of it hot'.

All we are offering her as a Christmas gift is a scented candle.

Monday 18 December
A civil letter arrived this morning, five days after posting, from Mrs Virginia Bottomley, Secretary of State for National Heritage. I had written to her recently about the plight of a large number of drama students who have had their grant aids withdrawn before completing their course. This seems to me monstrously unfair and an unwarrantable hardship. They are thrown out, only partially trained, into a tough, overcrowded profession where their chances of survival are almost nil. Those with parents who can afford the high fees are not going to have an easy time either, but for the good of the theatre of the future talent needs to be drawn from all sections of society. Mrs Bottomley grasps the situation but is puzzled as to what to do about it. Something, pray God.

Spent an hour this afternoon painting a mask at the request of the Prince's Trust; to be auctioned with hundreds of others next year. The charity sent me the mask and a little box of acrylic paints. I rather looked forward to doing it, spending a childish afternoon with my head on one side and splashing my paintbrush in a mug of water. In fact I found it hellish, and the result looks like something slapdash and insane done by Marie Laurencin. In despair I gave it a golden stubble from a Super Color Pen (also supplied by the trust) which advertises that it contains no xylene. What on earth is xylene? It could be a useful Scrabble word.

Wednesday 20 December
Drizzle much of the day. Tired of the low grey skies we are having. The past eight weeks have been a strain, so I decided to comfort myself with a Christmas present and went to Mr Blumlein's excellent little CD shop in Petersfield, where I treated myself to some Mozart, Shostakovich, Nielsen, Saint-Saëns and Medtner. The last was a mistake—he goes on too long, like an after-dinner speaker with a few good anecdotes but who doesn't know when to stop. Also got 'Dixieland' by the Dixieland Stompers—which I hope will encourage Merula to throw away Zimmer and crutches.

M said I was not to get her anything for Christmas (we both say the same thing every year and mean it) and I agreed; but I couldn't resist an exceptionally attractive, large, French breakfast cup and saucer. It's rather like the yellow tableware in Monet's dining-room at Giverny. I couldn't live with all that yellow or eat off it but a few pieces are almost exhilarating.

Back to Trollope. Have started *Cousin Henry*, one of the handful I've never read. It's not much longer than a novella but should see me over Christmas. I am always ashamed of the slowness of my reading. I think that it stems (apart from slowness of the brain) from that fact that when I come across dialogue in a novel I can't resist treating it as the text of a play and acting it out, with significant pauses and all.

Tuesday 26 December

Christmas was pleasantly quiet. The most enjoyable half hour was spent watching Wallace and Gromit. I want another short of them in about a month's time—but no imitators, please.

Our parish priest, Mgr Murtagh, kindly arranged things so that M could come to Midnight Mass avoiding the steps up to the church by using the sacristy. She can't cope yet with stairs. As always for Midnight Mass the place was crowded. The singing of the choir was somewhat elaborate but refreshingly vigorous. I spotted that my fly was unzipped when giving voice to 'Silent Night', a sure sign of advanced age in the male of the species. But it happened once long ago I remember. An anxious-looking lady followed me relentlessly down a street; I tried to shake her off by suddenly crossing the road, pretending to look in a reject china shop. Nothing deterred her. Her reflection was right beside me in the plate-glass window. 'Mr Guinness,' she whispered dramatically, 'your buttons are undone.'

I vote strongly for the royal yacht *Britannia* being kept in service. There was an interesting documentary TV about her last week. She looks good and it feels good. Why do so many people take a swipe at her, complaining that she is only kept going at 'the taxpayer's expense'? *Everything* is at the taxpayer's expense—or the tax-borrower's expense. *Britannia* seems to me excellent value in all her capacities and a fitting vessel for HM The Queen. She looks smart, as does her crew, and there were mercifully no shots of sailors going ashore in drag.

Reread a number of poems from John Updike's collection, *Facing Nature*. He is provocative and stimulating. There can't be many better novelists alive and yet it is somehow surprising to realize what a good poet he is.

Our good friend Henryetta Edwards came, as often in the past, to share our Christmas duck (or rather the stuffing and oddments, as she is a vegetarian). She is the daughter of Henry Edwards and Chrissie White, England's most popular romantic film stars of the silent era: *The Flag Lieutenant, Possession* and dozens of other successes. They were a beautiful, sweet-natured couple. He made a very brief, distinguished appearance in Ronald Neame's film of *The Card*. I saw it two years ago, the first time since the fifties. It was a lot better than I had remembered it and apart from a lousy attempt at a Potteries accent I didn't think I was too bad. Well, that's a nice change.

Wednesday 27 December
Tried telephoning Phyllida Law in her Argyllshire glen, fearing the blizzards that are causing havoc in Scotland may have drifted up to her rooftop. Couldn't get through. At first I had the BT ladylike voice politely and precisely telling me 'the number you have dialled has not been recognized the number you have dialled has not been recognized'—OK, OK, I had dialled the wrong bloody code—so I tried again, only to be greeted by something totally incomprehensible, sounding like Gaelic in a high wind. I think the words, rapidly reeled off, were part of a mathematical conundrum which may have ended with 'and now take away the number you first thought of'. I abandoned Phyllida to her fate. Her daughters, Emma and Sophie Thompson, will rescue her if need be. I can hear Phyllida's shrieks of delight should she be winched to safety.

A repeat of Wallace and Gromit in 'The Wrong Trousers' was a bonus to the day.

Where is all this global warming we read about? The fish lie low and still in the pond, covered by a layer of plate-glass ice. Only very few birds coming for nuts and seed. A puzzle.

Saturday 30 December
Freezing rain fell at about nine and within ten minutes we were marooned. The drive is a sheet of ice and the short incline up to it from the road is impassable. Mr Turrell, who occupies a small flat attached to the house and does a few kindly chores for us, took our van to Liss to collect Calor gas cylinders shortly before the sudden freeze hit. He couldn't get the van back to the gate. It is lodged under the bridge carrying the new A3—a stone's throw away— and there it will have to stay until there is something like a thaw. I never thought I would bless the A3 for its uses.

Naturally we have had to cancel going to dinner with our neighbours and naval friends, the Parkers. On New Year's Eve we shall batten down the hatches, close the scuttles and fasten tight the deadlights; then we shall consider ourselves well prepared for the dawn of 1996.

Sunday 31 December
'Is the piecing out of an old man's life worth the pains?' Found that in a pretty little copy of *Elia* given me by Mu Richardson. The answer is 'No! Certainly not!'—but yet I continue to do it.

A New Year Resolution which surely I can

keep: to greet each day with a verse from the Psalms, 'Cause me to hear thy loving-kindness in the morning.'

Should I ever act again (the idea doesn't much appeal) it would be cheering to remember a verse from another Psalm, 'The lines are fallen unto me in pleasant places.' Yet there would be small hope of me remembering the lines. And most rehearsal rooms are dispiriting. Such things were better catered for in the old days when you usually worked on the stage you were to appear on.

We watched the Australian film *Strictly Ballroom* for the third time and found it as enjoyable as ever. The credits slip by so swiftly, and in such small print, that I always miss the name of the actor/dancer who plays the boy's father. All the acting is lovely but his performance is wonderfully subtle and true. All I need now to make me happy looking at the box is a showing of the Swedish film *My Life as a Dog*.

And so we say goodbye to 1995; and I mean *goodbye* and not *arrivederci* etc., etc. It has had some good moments, but too many deaths and personal anxieties. Shalom. Shalom.

JANUARY 1996

Tuesday 2 January
1996 seeped in with enveloping mist which lasted most of the day. I remembered my New Year Resolution—'Cause me to hear thy loving-kindness in the morning' (Psalm 143) and I remembered again today.

Last night Blake Parker collected us for dinner. An enjoyable evening, chatting mostly of travel and of the morality, immorality, necessity or foolishness, wisdom or cunning of changing your political allegiance in midstream without advising your government bosses. The woman's name escapes me momentarily. I suppose it will get dinned into us. She will probably win her by-election when it occurs but, for the sake of her soul, I hope not with the stratospheric majority she predicted on the radio today. More seriously, we discussed the paper games we used to play at this time of the year when young. No swapping to opposite teams in mid game then.

Yesterday and today we had our favourite winter pre-lunch drink, my version of a Danish Mary. Clamato juice, Aalborg's akvavit, a flick of tabasco and a dribble of balsamic vinegar put in the whizzer with a cube or two of ice for a few seconds, just long enough to make a little froth on top. It makes a good excuse for doing whatever you want to do for the rest of the day.

Wednesday 3 January
A pleasing letter this morning from Miriam Rothschild saying that if we encounter each other this year (which I very much hope we may) she will tell me a romantic story about worms. Also she will bring me up to date on the minute creature that lives under the eyelids of the hippopotamus and feeds on its tears. Can't wait. I first met her at one of Dame Drue Heinz's fabulous summer parties; here's cadging an invitation to the next one.

This morning I found the oldest inhabitant of our pond, a fairly large koi carp, dead on the bottom. He had changed colour in death from gold, red and black to a pale red with tarnished silver scales. Not having been up to the pond for a few days I don't know how long he had been lying there. There was no sign of any damage to him; I am always a bit scared when the herons are about. At the moment there are eight near by.

Telephoned my dentist for a routine appointment. His secretary, who I think must be new, greeted me with 'Hi!' I felt I could only respond with 'Ho! and hum!' Now I think of it, I suppose I could have acknowledged her with, 'I answer "to 'Hi!' or to any loud cry,/Such as 'Fry me!' or 'Fritter my wig!'"' But then I might have been accused of uttering obscenities.

106

Thursday 4 January
We decided it would make a healthy change for M if we went to Bosham (a short way southwest of Chichester) for lunch. So David Pike, who has been taking me up to London and back for a long time—in fact ever since my third hernia operation, after which I decided lugging suitcases at railway stations was no longer for me—drove us to the Millstream Hotel for lunch. Keith Baxter, who lives in Bosham with his sweet dog Charlie, joined us. After lunch, the tide being well out, we went down to the hard and M had her chance to swing along on crutches in the bitterly cold, sea-smelling wind. Everything a pale grey except for a few white geese far off. Ten minutes was enough for all of us. It did M a lot of good.

Back home I lit the fire and settled down to Jane Austen's novella, *Lady Susan*. I wanted to know if this was the first story in Eng. Lit. told entirely in the form of letters, then I remembered Richardson's novels, *Pamela* and *Clarissa*.

Saturday 6 January
Epiphany and Twelfth Night. This used to be a great party-giving night, particularly in some theatre circles. Perhaps it still is. Down here there are only Merula, Alan B and me to celebrate by doing nothing. The best 12th Nt

parties I ever attended were given by Richard Leech and his family—a fairly violent but joyful playing of indoor games. One of the silliest and most intimate of games was the race between two teams passing an orange, held under the chin, from one chin to the next. In those days I had a sort of part-time secretary, a jolly lady who undoubtedly had more than one chin. I fear she was a liability to whichever team had the good nature and misfortune to choose her.

The Twelfth Night parties at the Old Vic before the war were memorable in a rather staid sort of way. At the end of the performance of whatever play we were performing a vast cake was brought on stage and the audience invited to partake of it. Lilian Baylis, who was the boss of the theatre, appeared in academic cap and gown to supervise the cutting up, and the actors, in full warpaint, distributed mean, crumbly pieces to the bemused and hungry. We felt like the disciples handing out bits of loaves and fishes. And, sure enough, someone was bound to sing 'When that I was and a little tiny boy' from the end of *Twelfth Night*. The best rendering of that song that I have heard, not vocally, but dramatically, was in Peter Hall's production at the Playhouse a few years back. The Feste used his tambourine as if raindrops were beginning to fall, starting with a few slow, heavy drops, such as we often experience at the end of summer, and then increasing in intensity with the feel of winter. You almost turned up your coat collar for protection. The actor was only drumming with his fingers under the tambourine, but it was magic.

In 1937 Guthrie directed *Twelfth Night* at the Old Vic with Larry Olivier as Toby Belch, his then wife, Jill Esmond, as Olivia and the adorable Jessica Tandy as Viola. Marius Goring was Feste and I was Aguecheek; for some odd quirky reason of my own I played him as if he were Stan Laurel. It was a very undisciplined affair, not good at all, but I was thrilled to be acting my first important part. Also I learned a thing or two while doing it. Like every Aguecheek that has ever been I got a laugh on the line, 'I was adored once too.' One midweek matinee, with a sparse audience, no laugh came although I undoubtedly sought it. Larry hissed in my ear, 'Fool! You should know a matinee audience would never laugh at that.' When I played Malvolio in a poor TV of *Twelfth Night* Larry came to the final run-through (Joan Plowright, Lady Olivier, was giving her Viola). Just before we went on air he said to me, 'Marvellous, old cock! I never realized Malvolio could be played as a bore.' Such-like encouragements were part of his repertoire. Yet I was fond of him.

In 1948 the Old Vic management invited me, at a week's notice, to direct the play at the New Theatre (now the Albery). It had been already cast and the sets and costumes designed. All that was required of me, really, was to stage-manage it and make suggestions to the actors. I should have refused—insufficient time to prepare—but I was anxious to test out if I could *help* actors and if they would trust me. It was a rather lame affair, and I disliked the sets and costumes, but I think I succeeded with two or three of the cast. Not with the Viola; she simply had to go before we opened in London and another one had to be found.

The most exciting performance of the play I have ever seen was Playfair's black-and-white production in the early thirties. *Everything* (setting, costumes) was black and white, with the exception of Malvolio's yellow stockings. Jean Forbes-Robertson was Viola; a breathtaking piece of acting, exuding purity, clarity, imagination and a sweet-sad love. Arthur Wontner presented a chilling, formidable, malevolent Malvolio. Quite the funniest Malvolio I've seen was Paul Rogers but I can't remember anything else about the evening.

So much for *Twelfth Night*, loveliest of plays. It being Epiphany we packed up the Christmas cards and put the crib back in its cake tin until next year. A crib? Well, not exactly; the Holy Family, Wise Men and Shepherds all made of small Peruvian gourds and very solemnly painted, all with wide staring eyes.

Oh, yes, and I have won something on the Lottery; three of my numbers came up so I suppose I can claim £10. Forty million pounds are knocking around somewhere. Clergy who run whist drives and raffles are snarling at the immorality of it all.

Tuesday 9 January
Tried telephoning Ed Herrmann but he was rashly out shopping in the New York State blizzard which is raging. Managed to get through with ease to Anne Kaufman Schneider in Manhattan, who said the snow is practically up to one's armpits. She says it's all very pretty to look at but whenever she gazes out of the window of her Madison Avenue apartment she sees people falling down smack. Apparently it is eerily quiet; no traffic.

Anne and Irving are now my oldest and certainly closest American friends. The connection was made many years ago through Anne's stepmother, Leueen MacGrath, who was at one time married to George Kaufman; she was a very dear intimate friend. The Schneiders arrive in London next week and make for Manchester, where her father's play, *Animal Crackers*, is a big success. We shall meet on Wednesday for lunch; this has become a ritual, to meet up the day after their arrival. It is the same when I go to New York. Arriving as I always do in the morning we arrange to lunch at Jean Lafite on W 58th Street. I sadly wonder if that will ever happen again. We have had marvellous holidays together, notably in Greece and also in Paris. Oh, the world is wide open still, but the transatlantic haul is getting an effort. I would rather potter around Europe.

A daffodil is a few inches high; too early. The days are drawing out quite noticeably, but I continue to wonder where all the birds are. A robin keeps an occasional eye on me in my study and a blackbird digs around and looks askance—and that's all. Even our faithful crow doesn't turn up. When the weather was bitter I put out several lumps of fat but they lie untouched.

Thursday 11 January
General Sir Peter de la Billière, who commanded so admirably in the Gulf War and gave us all much needed confidence, said in a BBC interview a few days ago that senior figures in the Ministry of Defence had insisted on a low-flying policy, of which he gravely disapproved and which he protested against. It seems it was a policy that resulted in heavy casualties on our side. Today, it appears, he has had to apologize, which is a pity. Surely the apology should come from the MoD for unnecessary loss of life and aircraft. It sounds to me rather like the face-saving we have been told happened way behind the lines in the 1914–18 war. 'Gentlemanly agreements' in

high places are usually suspect.

Go on, General, withdraw your apology; stick to your guns, even if now they are only moral ones.

In the evening listened to recording of *Manon Lescaut* (Tebaldi, Monaco). A great pleasure for me, but I always think M wrinkles her nose slightly at Puccini.

Friday 12 January
Chechen fighters, holding about a hundred hostages in buses, are now surrounded by Russian army units. All very ugly and disturbing. We seem to be back to square one. Four young Cambridge scientists are being held hostage in a remote part of Indonesia. No recent news of hostages held in Kashmir. Our passports still have the preamble, 'Her Britannic Majesty's Secretary of State Requests and requires in the Name of Her Majesty all those whom it may concern to allow the bearer to pass freely without let or hindrance and to afford the bearer such assistance and protection as may be necessary.' Unsigned. In the old days there were important-looking signatures—like Bevin's. I am afraid all the flourishes of Capital Letters don't mean as much as a Victorian pop-pop gunboat.

At home the year has started vigorously, with serial killers, strangulations, knifings (very popular with adolescents) and the daily clutch of muggings.

Lady Thatcher looked radiantly aggressive on the box making a speech about One Nation and No Nation. I admit I don't quite understand what it all means; or why owning your own home, if you are one of the lucky ones, makes you a One Nation person. Disraeli, we are told, talked of Two Nations—rich and poor—but now I read he never got round to One Nation. On good authority we have been informed that the poor will be with us always. Obviously it is our duty to try to help all we can (without becoming Mrs Jellybys)—but I could do without advertising slogans and 'sound bites'.

Court, Cloister and City: The Art and Culture of Central Europe, 1450–1800, by Thomas Da Costa Kaufmann has arrived from Heywood Hill. It has been highly recommended by a friend and I look forward to it, but it is another of those books too heavy to hold in bed, where I like to read. A quick glance at its dozens of interesting photographs and I kick myself for not having kept my eyes wide open, or made proper inquiries about everything when in Prague, Munich, Einsiedeln, Berlin or almost anywhere I have travelled. Usually I have felt too embarrassed to show my ignorance by asking. Idiotic pride, of course, and a hang-up from schooldays—mustn't stand out from the rest by showing interest.

Tuesday 16 January
Came up to town yesterday morning, giving a lift to Jill Balcon. Rather slow, misty journey. Bank, haircut; then to Conran's shop in the old Michelin building and bought a very comfortable, black leather armchair. For years I have been without a cosy chair in which to relax or doze off; this fits the bill well. As it should at £1,100. M will kill me, the cat will scratch it to bits and now that I have ordered it I fear it may look rather funereal; but it is not too large and the arms are easy. At Conran's my eye also fell on a handsome sofa but that had better wait a few weeks as I know M will resist it. I somehow have to woo her away from her present bedsitter attitude—grubby loose covers and nests of wool. She likes going to bed with the fire still flickering.

Took Nicola Pagett and her husband Graham Swannell to dinner at L'Incontro, which is as good as ever. Nicola banged on happily about the prospects for Tony Blair— like an old friend of mine who announced she would follow Lawrence of Arabia to the ends of the world—but Graham played it cooler. An enjoyable evening.

* * *

Well, my bad eye has to be taken to Moorfields Eye Hospital for some sort of sonic test, as it is now thought the retina has become detached or perforated or is anyway not up to much good. That will be next Tuesday. On the result they will decide whether to operate or not. As they can't restore my sight it seems a rather pointless exercise. Oh, and my right eye has an infection, which I didn't know, but that can be dealt with by drops.

Bought Barry Humphries' novel *Women in the Background*. Loved his autobiography and enjoy his enthusiasm for, among others, Charles Conder. Two or three years ago I spotted a Conder oil painting I longed for. The price was formidable. It purported to be of a small Mediterranean port—very colourful and it had a Spanish or Italian feel to it, but I was anxious about a cart in the foreground which clearly had elliptical wheels: a bumpy ride for someone. I *still* might have taken a deep breath, braved my bank manager's frown, and bought it; but I was saved by spotting that the harbour wall had a tide mark of at least five feet. This was no *Mediterranean* port. In fact it was all a delightful fabrication but not within the clasp of the Pillars of Hercules. I'd like to have it all the same, for its freshness and the feel of the paint.

Thursday 18 January
Returned from London Wednesday afternoon. Really, I must not complain about, or even mention my silly eye: yesterday I gave

lunch to the Schneiders and Irving's sight is terrible. It has been so for a few years and, after various operations, it gets no better but he never grumbles—just misses his wine glass by an inch or two.

The house has been looking drab so I went to Pulbrook & Gould, whose flowers are always fresh and appealing, and bought a quantity of tulips, mimosa, hyacinths and bright anemones. Now all is fragrant and attractive; or at least the living-room looks less like a bedsit in spite of M's bed in one corner. Next week, perhaps, she may be able to manage the stairs.

The Blake Parkers came to dinner and M excelled herself in the kitchen, providing a light, creamy, mildly curried chicken. It was from a recipe given her by Vincent Sardi, of Sardi's Restaurant, when I was doing Eliot's *The Cocktail Party* in New York in 1951. She had stuck to it rigidly through the years.

The new armchair has arrived and I generously invited the gallant captain to use it for the evening. It is very comfortable but a touch of effort is needed to get out of it. Funnily enough Merula approves. I've put one of her wool needlework cushions on it, which shows up brilliantly, like a Bonnard framed in a fat, soft, black leather frame, if one can imagine such a thing.

Incense in Coventry Cathedral (if they ever used it) has given way to petrol fumes. A car was driven up the nave; the Bishop, in full ecclesiastical rig, was celebrating the car industry. In the midst of it all a latter-day Lady Godiva flung off her fur coat to reveal herself in the nude with anti-internal-combustion slogans painted all over her. She was *not* protesting, I think, about the desecration of the cathedral but against the use of cars in general. Perhaps Lady Godiva isn't the right image; after all, the real Lady Godiva spread her hair around and hoped not to be seen naked as she rode throught the streets. Well, that was in the middle of the eleventh century and legend has it that the people of Coventry confined themselves to their houses so as not to embarrass her. Today, of course, they might watch her furtively on TV or, more likely, throng the streets to egg her on. And she wouldn't turn a hair.

I recall how outraged the civilized world was at the bombing of Coventry Cathedral by the Nazis in 1941. 'Desecration!' we all cried. 'Savages!' I am not sure that I would feel so strongly today.

Saturday 20 January
A letter this morning from Alexander Walker, film critic of the *Evening Standard*, enclosing a copy of his review of *Silent Witness*—a title new to me and rather a good one. (I looked up my diary entry for 21 February last year where I state I had received a decent mention, in a Hollywood trade paper, for a part I had never

played in a film I had never heard of.) Walker's letter said I was in the film, billed as a 'Guest Mystery Star', and the penny dropped. Searching though old diaries I came across March 1985, almost eleven years ago, when I was in Hamburg, very briefly, to receive the Stiftung Shakespeare prize. On the evening of 21 March I attended a party given by the British Council, mostly for drama and film students, where I was introduced to a serious-looking, passionate, would-be director, Anthony Waller, who was beginning work—in fits and starts—on a film he hoped to finish one distant day. Back at my hotel (The Atlantic) I dined with Julian Glover and suddenly the young man appeared. He asked me if I would say three or four lines in his film, as a sort of Mafia chief. I pointed out that it was nearly midnight and that I was flying back to England in the morning. He looked desperate. He could *shoot* me, he said, at 07.30 in the morning. (He didn't tell me the film was about the making of snuff movies—just that it was a thriller and contained nothing pornographic.) I was pretty sure there was no clear plot and I asked to see the script. He disappeared, into the hotel lobby I think, and returned a few minutes later with three or four lines of dialogue, hot off his portable typewriter I guess. The lines meant nothing to be and he couldn't explain much, but there was something about his personality and determination which impressed me. In some ways he reminded me of the much lamented Robert Hamer (*Kind Hearts and Coronets*) but without, as yet, Robert's sophistication or dry wit. So I said I'd do it, but if he hadn't finished with me by 08.30 I'd just walk away, and I meant that. So at 07.45, sitting in the back of a chauffeur-driven car in a nearby underground garage, I said my incomprehensible lines to a non-existent actor and was finished on time. And that was that. Naturally I took no money (nor was I offered any, it being, as I thought, all student work) but I made one stipulation—that my name should not appear on the cast list or in any publicity. When I got home letters to this effect were exchanged between us. After ten years the film was completed and shown, fairly successfully, in the USA. As a professional film. And now it is here, with its Mystery Star, who had forgotten all about it.

Mr Waller, I predict, will go far; but it may take him time.

Monday 23 January
Have abandoned *Court, Cloister and City* as being too indigestible for me. Besides, the weight is too heavy on my tummy and the paper too shiny for my eyes. So I am afraid I am going to remain dismally ignorant about art and architecture in eastern Europe. The Barry Humphries book I am finding very funny; it is not a recommended Christmas

present for Terence Rattigan's Aunt Edna, should she be still alive. When I have finished it I shall plunge back into the Kilmartin translation of Proust: the footnotes are so good. During the war I had the old Scott Moncrieff edition in my ship; twelve handy blue volumes, which would fit neatly into the pocket of a duffle coat. I only read the whole work once at that time. It seemed so very remote. Proust calls for a hammock in a garden, plenty of cushions and a long summer drink at your side; pleasant excuses to doze off now and then. He didn't go so well with the smell of diesel oil, with the smacking of waves against the ship's side, nor with the strident bell sounding off the watch.

Today there is much fuss about Harriet Harman, of the Shadow Cabinet, sending her eleven-year-old son to St Olave's School in what the media describe as 'leafy Orpington'. Presumably it is not very leafy at this time of year. Part of the trouble is that the boy has to take an exam and face an interview. Without such things I can't see how the school would know in what form to place him. Neither do I see why all the emphasis is put on Ms Harman's decision; presumably her husband should have at least a 50 per cent say in the matter, and perhaps Master Joseph may have views on his education.

Penguin Books got in touch this morning to say they might like to do a hardback reissue of my book of memoirs, *Blessings in Disguise*, published by Hamish Hamilton in 1985, and asking if there are any alterations I would like to make. There are two or three factual errors I would wish to correct and I must remove a thoughtless unkindness about someone. Also, if everyone concerned feels it is OK, I would like to include most of a chapter I removed shortly before publication. This was partly because I was reluctant to hurt the feelings of an old lady whom I admired, but also I didn't wish to risk any legal action. It all had to do with snake poison which, I maintain, must have been put in my food when lunching with Dame Freya Stark in Asolo in 1954. Freya has long gone to her Maker and the story is now, I hope, just a funny one. I can't pretend I am not chuffed by the idea of re-publication. And, of course, at being alive.

Tuesday 24 January
To London; to Moorfields Eye Hospital in the afternoon. A charming white-haired lady ran some sort of sonic pencil over my left eyelid and came up with remarkable pictures, which were quite meaningless to me, looking as they did like nebulae on the outer confines of *Star Wars*. She said that as far as she could tell the retina hasn't been damaged, which is marvellous. The pictures are now being sent to the specialist and he will decide whether to operate to clear away the sloppy blood in the

jelly of the eye. I shall know more soon. The car taking me to Moorfields wriggled its way through tiny, twisted City streets which were almost deserted; a few thin clerks with blue noses hunched themselves against the bitter wind, walking stiffly and alone, like the black matchstick figures in a Lowry industrial townscape. The women to be seen were, for the most part, dressed as Paddington Bear. It is a pleasing hat but the face peeping from underneath it should be under thirty. The car slid past St Paul's Cathedral which somehow looked smaller than usual and rather drab. Elizabeth Frink's sheep, nearby, are being *driven* by their shepherd, as was pointed out to me a few years ago, and not *following* him as the Bible recommends. Things are out of joint.

The last time I was at St Paul's was for David Lean's memorial service, which was a big production number, with a military band outside on the steps playing 'Colonel Bogey', as used in the film of *The Bridge on the River Kwai*. Inside it was film star studded, at least under the dome. I don't think people at the back were totally aware of what was going on or why. Compromise is my middle name so I sat myself between the two groups. (TV images of royal weddings passed before my eyes; particularly of the Duchess of York's wedding-dress, which seemed to spread and spread like 'silly putty', the substance greatly prized by children in the early fifties. Did it rustle or slide silently?) Melvyn Bragg gave an admirable address, beautifully spoken; he managed to get in a snide remark of David's about me which caused a few discreet titters. The titterers were sitting, of course, directly under the Whispering Gallery. 'Titter you not!' as Frankie Howerd used to say. I had to balance my thoughts as best I could, pushing aside my bad recollections of David's extreme unpleasantness in latter years but remembering the enchanting, affable, exciting man he was in the days of making *Great Expectations* and *Oliver Twist*. He could still switch on the charm even in his last years but I had grown mistrustful of it. We each did our best, I think, to repair our damaged friendship but it didn't really work out. I needed someone with whom I could laugh (not David's strongest point) and he depended so much, it seemed to me, on sycophants. But he was marvellously generous with his riches. The car left St Paul's behind in the fading light. I wished David eternal happiness, as I have always done since the day he died.

Inside Moorfields dozens of black people were sitting, patient and forlorn, on ranks of coloured plastic chairs. They all had glaucoma, or so the signs on the walls led me to assume. I was happy to be going to my sonic experience, which seemed more glamorous.

Spent a merry evening with my old actor friend Richard Leech. (He is the only actor I know who enjoys dressing as an actor laddie—very wide brimmed velour hat, fancy waistcoat and heavy gold watch-chain.) The poor fellow has got very deaf but he lip-reads superbly well. Funnily enough he is the best 'hearer of lines' I've come across. He knows exactly when to be insistently precise and when to let things slide to create confidence. Also, he always chuckles at the funny bits, which is encouraging when you have secret doubts about the script.

Saturday 27 January
Marriott White had invited us to join her in her box at the Albert Hall last night to see Cirque de Soleil. Very much wanted to go but we felt it would be unwise to accept—M's doubtful capacity for climbing stairs yet, the likely scrimmage getting in and out of the building, the reported psychedelic lighting effects which I might find nauseating, and the high decibel count of the music which would deafen us both. The rickety little chairs in the Albert Hall boxes for 2¾ hours were offputting as well. So a rich opportunity has been missed through the tiresomeness of age and accident.

Tonight we were to have given a small dinner party but we woke this morning to a white world and snow still falling. Roads were reported to be hazardous so we thought it unfair on guests and cancelled. I just wish I hadn't taken the magnificent Roux cake/dessert out of the deep freeze; it will have to be eaten during the next two or three days.

Hand-basins upstairs have frozen. Boiling kettles, candle flames—no good. Fingers crossed that when the thaw comes it doesn't bring with it burst pipes. This house is ridiculous; nearly all pipes are exposed to northern and eastern weather. I would like a sheltered cottage.

Can't remember where I came across this description of someone's Wiltshire cottage: 'Simply divine, covered in roses and smothered in hysteria.'

Monday 29 January
'The bawdy hand of the dial is now upon the prick of noon'—but no sign of our expected but unknown guest, who is half an hour late. It is hoped that he may arrange a small exhibition of Merula's paintings and/or wool pictures. He is probably lost in the narrow roads under the Hangers; unless he is taking a short rest, as is now obligatory by a Brussels ruling for shellfish travelling more than thirty-five miles. The Walrus and the Carpenter might get into hot legal and political trouble today. 'I put it to you, sir, that you failed to assure yourself that the dozen oysters were properly rested before you ate them.'

*   *   *

The young man finally turned up and was very

agreeable, bright, intelligent and amusing.

Sent back three lots of junk mail asking the firms concerned to remove my name from their mailing lists but I expect they won't bother. Two of the unwanted intrusions sought to over-excite me by saying my name had been chosen to be eligible for a huge cash prize or failing that a flashy car. The third glossy letter wanted to send someone to advise me how to save money for my old age. A bit late for such advice. I was not impressed at my name being incorrectly spelled or—if I dare mention such a thing these days—without my splendid accolade. Almost every letter marked Private, Confidential or Personal makes its way pretty swiftly to the waste-paper basket.

FEBRUARY 1996

Thursday 1 February
Pale sunshine all day: quite a lot of frost.

Most MPs are putting out feelers for more pay; a few suggesting that double their present salaries would be acceptable. Rather a lot, I think, for so much yah-booing. Could not a scheme be devised whereby MPs were paid for by those who voted for them but not, of course, by those who opposed their election? It would make for an interesting disparity of rewards. A letter in today's *Telegraph* points out that the US House of Representatives has only 435 members for a country with about five times our population. Perhaps we could get along quite well with only 300 representatives. Now *there* would be an economy.

Last night we watched, aghast, a TV programme about American mothers training their tiny-tot little girls in the arts of seduction for a glitzy appearance at the Southern Charm Pageant in Atlanta, Georgia. As rabid 'stage mothers' they made our own appalling breed of ambitious mums seem only partially insane. I think the five-year-old winner, crowned in a tinselly way, was hailed as 'Queen of Queens'. I dread to think of her future.

Something in the programme reminded me of my brilliant friend Peter Glenville holding an audition, many years ago, for the small part of a girl in a Feydeau farce. Both the girl who presented herself and the garrulous mother were total strangers to the aspirate 'h'. Peter got so confused listening to them that he heard himself saying, '''As she hactually 'ad hany hacting experience?'

Saturday 3 February
A couple of evenings ago I was thinking of Peter Glenville, whom I haven't been in touch with for a few months, wondering if he was all right and whether he was in Mexico, where he spends much of the year, or in New York. Yesterday morning, only half awake, I found myself trying to complete and place the line which begins, 'Her voice was ever soft.' Of course I know it backwards—

> Her voice was ever soft,
> Gentle and low, an excellent thing in
>   woman.

It is spoken by Lear of Cordelia at the end of the play. It was a trivial thing and I soon put it from my mind. In the late afternoon Peter telephoned me from New York, asking what I was up to, etc. I told him that, among other things, I was going to London next week to consult an ear specialist as I suspect I need a hearing-aid. 'It's women's voices,' I said, 'with which I have difficulty; particularly if they are high-pitched.' Peter commented by saying, 'You'd have something to complain about if you lived in NY. There is no question of women here being like Cordelia, with soft, gentle and low voices.' It was a nothing, as is apparent, but yet these odd tiny coincidences and nearly telepathic experiences continue to puzzle and intrigue.

A few years ago the aircraft I had boarded at Kennedy Airport for a flight home was aborted in its take-off just before leaving the runway. It came to a juddering halt and all passengers were instructed to return to the departure lounge. Within two minutes of getting there I heard my name called over the loud-speaker saying there was an urgent telephone call for me. When I got to the telephone I heard Peter, who was in Manhattan, saying, 'Thank God you are still there! Whatever you do don't get on that plane. I had a strong premonition ten minutes ago that it would crash.' He begged me not to get on the next flight either but to return to his apartment and go home another day. I said that if I started obeying such hunches I would probably never fly again, and I caught the next available flight.

Matthew came to lunch. He is off to Bulgaria in a week's time for a skiing holiday. Foolhardy, in my opinion, considering he fell off a horse two weeks ago and shook up an eye rather alarmingly. Now he is in the grip of goggles, woolly, bobbled hats and so on but can't yet say Yes, No, Please or Thank You in Bulgarian, let alone 'Take me to your Chief Medicine Man.'

Monday 5 February
An invitation this morning to attend a charity dinner and 'entertain us for half an hour afterwards'. The wrong invitee. Suggest they approach Peter Ustinov for a very up-market appeal, but if it is in the opposite direction then maybe Ruby Wax.

It seems an impertinence, when pushing eighty-two, to deliberately associate with people a lot younger than oneself, feeling that possibly one might interest or entertain them. Of course it isn't quite that: secretly one hopes and longs to draw on the vitality and brightness of the young, and above all to be able to join in their laughter. How is one to grasp the all-pervasiveness of time? Somewhere Einstein wrote, 'The distinction between past, present and future is only an illusion, however persistent.' Any comment from me would be a gem for Pseuds' Corner. But how does Einstein's statement compare with St Augustine, who quoted, with admiration, an old man he knew?—'Time comes from the future, which does not yet exist, into the present which has no duration, and goes in to the past, which has ceased to exist.'

To entertain for half an hour? Sadly, I have

no conjuring tricks, no stories with a *double entendre* to double them up with guffaws, nor any political or social tub to thump; also I am a lousy speaker, either too brief (which sounds bleak) or a meaningless rambler (which is just boringly embarrassing). I wonder whose after-dinner speeches, in history, have been most dreaded? Socrates went on and on but at least he kept his young fellow diners wide awake by catching them out with trick questions. St Paul probably took some beating; I sometimes think with compassion of Master Eutychus who succumbed to deep sleep when St P talked all evening until midnight and the poor boy fell backwards out of a third-storey window. They all blamed the heat of the burning lamps but I have an idea that was just a polite excuse—St P had gone on far too long.

Of course you don't have to go back almost two thousand years to find people who bang on; they are right with us today.

In the summer of 1992 I was thrilled to receive an invitation to dine at the Admiralty, and a fine and marvellous occasion it was. We sat down fourteen to the table and in an adjacent room sailors played stringed instruments really well. When I arrived the Flag Lieutenant (for it was he) greeted me with 'So glad to see you!' and what I took to be a pleased smile of recognition. He invited me to see where I would be sitting. 'You are here,' he said, 'with Mr So-and-so on one side and

Admiral So-and-so on the other. Opposite you, Alec Guinness, the actor.' 'Ah!' I said, 'a Doppelgänger!' But he didn't get it. At the end of dinner our admiral host said, 'I think Lord Tonypandy would like to say a few words.' 'Yes, I certainly would,' said Lord Tonypandy (he had been elevated to the peerage that day) and away he went, in a very relaxed way. He spoke extremely well but after half an hour wrist-watches were being looked at, furtively, under the table. After an hour no one had the temerity to cry out 'Order! Order!' The chimes of midnight were sounding before our host came to the rescue with, 'I am sure we are all very grateful to our honoured guest.' 'Hear, hear!' etc., was rather muffled by the instant pushing back of chairs and the stretching of cramped limbs. No windows to fall from but lavs had to be found and taxis in Whitehall sought.

Tuesday 6 February
A sluggish journey to London through falling snow; after Guildford there was sunshine of a sort. Object of trip, to lunch at Wiltons with three Penguins to discuss publication of this diary and the reissue of *Blessings in Disguise* (a book of memoirs I put together in 1985). Talk of photographs for dust-covers of both books but I loathe being photographed and dug in my heels. I suggest for one of them, if the National Portrait Gallery will give permission, a

134

photograph of the head Elisabeth Frink did of me. It is very imperious, not much like me—suggesting a bull-necked Roman Emperor—but is obviously good work. For the other I think a photo of the head done a few years ago by Lucy Poett, which is very exact. With one of my hats on top, which it sometimes wears, it is disturbingly real.

The Piers Paul Reads for dinner. Enjoyable, but although the food was good the *sommelier* proved hard to contact. Once during the meal I had to track him down across the room and catch him by the elbow; he appeared to be mesmerized, listening vaguely to a table of businessmen.

Wednesday 7 February
There is a slightly odd letter from John Gielgud in the correspondence columns of today's *Telegraph*. He strikes a brief sad note about the burning down of the Fenice opera house but most of the letter is taken up with a description of a candlelit supper, given by rich Americans, at the Doria Palace. I can't find the connection between fire, candlelight and gondolas using a watery garage.

Had my left ear tested. Specialist advises me to invest in a hearing-aid. He would really like me to start a course of lip-reading but I'm too old a dog to learn.

Ever since he picked up the Speaker's mace in the House of Commons and brandished it, in 1977, I have kept a wary eye on Mr Heseltine. Now, as our Deputy Prime Minister, he is quoted as apparently approving the late payment of bills; a little jugglery with interest. This is a practice which has resulted in the ruin of too many small businesses, to my own knowledge, and caused great distress to struggling professionals. The mace-waving in 1977 was theatrically over the top; the endorsement in 1996 of delayed payment is surely morally below the belt.

To Heywood Hill bookshop and bought Ferdinand Mount's *Umbrella* and volume one of Admiral Lord Cochrane's *Autobiography of a Seaman*, first published in 1860.

Home tomorrow.

Saturday 10 February
Arrived back Thursday lunch-time loaded with a new desk lamp, dozens of candles, a pork pie, cheese and a very smart correspondence file, covered in royal blue cloth, which I had found at Conran's. The sun shone for a number of hours and a thaw has set in.

The big event yesterday was getting M's bed out of the living-room (two stalwart chaps heaved it upstairs) and a return to some semblance of decency. M rather sad to see her downstairs life disrupted but she has to admit things look better. And, oh, it's good to have a bit of space again. What's more, the windows have been cleaned in my absence. Perhaps my long-distance sight is not as bad as I thought.

A very brief, violent hailstorm this afternoon turned the drive crumbly white, scared the dogs stiff, amazed the cat and made me wonder if the windows might buckle. The suddenness and viciousness of it brought to mind the ghastly attack yesterday evening of the IRA in the Canary Wharf area.

I had a long letter this morning from the painter Keith Grant, who has just returned from one of his regular visits to Norway. When we first met, early last year, I told him I longed to see again aurora borealis. His description of what he saw this winter in the Arctic Circle is so good I hope he will allow me to quote it in full. Here it is:

The most dramatic display was on Christmas Eve. I was driving between two small towns about half an hour apart. Suddenly the sky to the east began to glow, a huge fan of green bluish light rose almost to zenith with mysterious dark patches of strange and irregular shapes within it. These were clouds in silhouette. The fan of light broke up into vertical shafts of light extending upwards from the horizon to a great height. They began to ripple and change position and then separated into so many hanging curtains, the lower edges of which were tinged deep crimson and rose colour. The main colour was a bright whitish green. The effect was exactly like an enormous stage with hanging curtains receding and diminishing in size to give the most awesome perspective expression of deep space. From this area in the east the whole heavens became a vast dome of hanging silken banners and flags. The movement of the ribbons of light was unnerving. It was as if some conscious agency was causing the waves and ripples of light, constantly shifting position so that no effect could be memorized, since it was eclipsed by a more and more stunning pageantry.

A great loop of light appeared and then seemed to descend towards me, only to rise and shrink with such rapidity I wondered if I had seen it or imagined it.

Suddenly it was over, a few fitful flashes here and there, and then the darkness and intense cold through which the stars (which I could see through the aurora), now no longer in competition with the northern lights, shone in diamond-like brilliance. A Norwegian girl said to me that when one sees the Aurora like this—'It is like nature's benediction.' Wonderful, wonderful. I have seen so many displays recently that I am satisfied.

Sunday 11 February
Snow and frost have gone and a thousand moles have come up for air, building monstrous turrets from which to sniff out the land. In fact probably only two or three of them but, like the IRA, they have done remarkable damage. Tomorrow I expect our Mrs Spurdle will pour Jeyes Fluid down the shafts to their tunnels; we have tried *everything* else over the years.

The sedge is well and truly withered and no birds sing. Even my confident robin and wary blackbird haven't put in an appearance for about a week.

No one can feel much like singing today, except, perhaps, some Irish terrorists and their subterranean supporters. There is a melancholy feel in the air, a weary 'I have been here before' attitude; the hopes of the past eighteen months irreparably dented, I fear.

I remember an English priest saying to me, years ago, 'I am sick of Irishmen coming to the confessional with the works of St John of the Cross in one pocket and a gun in the other.'

And now to Mass. There will be prayers for peace and justice as always. It's the interpretation of justice that causes the greatest difficulty.

Tuesday 13 February
A filthy cold. It started on Sunday, in a small scratchy way, and the bald dome of my head

got very chilled in church. I must get a skullcap for protection. It can't matter if people think me eccentric or a member of some strange lay order. I shall brave it out.

Have cancelled all my appointments in London for tomorrow and Thursday. Now I shall take myself to bed with a pile of books, if not to read at least to pick over. There are a few more pages of *Umbrella* to finish, and the Admiral Cochrane autobiography to start and, if I have the strength—using my knees as a book-rest—Montaigne's *Essays*. Montaigne is always a wonderful bed companion, particularly when you are feeling peevish and low. The *Essays* would be my Desert Island book above all others. Can't remember what I chose when the late Roy Plomley swooped down on me with all those screeching seagulls. Milton? A Dickens? He made me feel like discarded offal thrown over the stern of a ship, so I suppose I put the whole thing out of my mind and let it recede to a distant horizon; now it is out of sight.

Wednesday 14 February
A cold, bright, sunny St Valentine's day. A few pigeons cooing and the blackbird outside my study very busy but I don't think he is nest building. Two or three crocuses look as if they are about to flower. Snowdrops have been disappointing so far—only one vigorous clump. I am feeling better.

It is reported in the press (can it really be true?) that in the USA some states are considering legislation instructing schools to teach that the Potato Famine in Ireland in the 1840s was brought about by British attempts at genocide. It sounds as if this could be very unsubtle anti-American propaganda. If, however, it is truly reported, then it must be heavy-handed Boston/Irish anti-British propaganda. I was sufficiently irritated to look up some facts in reference books. The Potato Famine was experienced across most of Europe, although, of course, it was at its most devastating in Ireland. A decade earlier the turnip crops were ruined everywhere and in the 1850s vine mildew reduced the harvest of grapes by two thirds. You pick your decade and choose your famine. And that applies pretty well worldwide today. Political propaganda has deep, poisonous roots capable of blighting all our lives.

Sharman Douglas has died (daughter of the American ambassador to St James's who lost an eye in a fishing accident). I didn't know her at all well but liked her immensely. Merula and I rented a bungalow next to hers, down a rough, fir-tree-lined little cul-de-sac in a hilly part of Los Angeles. That was in 1961, when I was making a film called *A Majority of One*. (I don't think I ever saw more than ten minutes of it. It was Penelope Gilliatt, I think, who described my make-up as a Japanese business gent as me with ravioli stuck on my eyelids. That was the only thing about the whole enterprise that made me laugh.) Sharman Douglas was a marvellous, forthright, warm-hearted and funny neighbour.

The bungalow we rented belonged to Larry Harvey. It was a hideaway love-nest, I believe, and everything was white and gilt; white walls, white flooring, white furniture, white curtains, bedspreads, etc.—everything stuck together with gold, as one might have expected. Not the most restful colour scheme for Californian sunlight. But it did have a kidney-shaped swimming-pool which was the colour of turquoise and had dazzling underwater lighting. Really we were rather grateful for it. Our neighbours, Miss Douglas and Kate Smith (of Messrs W.H.) made us feel civilized.

Friday 16 February
A new John Updike novel—always something to look forward to with keen anticipation—arrived from New York this morning, a gift from Anne Kaufman Schneider. It was sensibly and smartly packaged by the admirable Madison Avenue Bookshop. The great Admiral Cochrane must drop anchor for a few days and await sailing orders. The Updike (*In the Beauty of the Lilies*) looks fairly substantial but mercifully it is not in the same league as the Scott inquiry report.

Yesterday M and I caught ourselves horribly stooped, hobbling and shuffling about the place. Well, it was rather cold. We straightened ourselves and I suggested we should change our name to Mr & Mrs Doubled-Upp. Invitations could go out, 'Mr & Mrs Doubled-Upp have pleasure in inviting you to bend over a cup of Royal Blend tea.' Oh, how foolish can one get?

A good-humoured, tough young man, wearing an earring remarkably like a curtain ring, came to make some adjustment to our Renault van, which has been behaving oddly. With a twisted bit of wire and a lot of lying on his back and stomach, getting filthy, which he seemed to enjoy, he did the trick. The van now purrs away merrily. I forgot to ask him if he'd like to clean up; he could have used Pulbrook & Gould's mighty expensive Gardener's Scrub which we are assured does wonders. He drove away in a spotless white car. It's heartening to come across young, interested, skilful, English workmen—and in this district we frequently do; and they are always bright and pleasant.

As the sun went down today it was reported that from Edinburgh to Manchester there was a very rare phenomenon to be seen—cloud clusters the colour of the spectrum about fifteen miles above the surface of the earth. It is believed they are formed by tiny particles of ice catching the last of the sun's rays. That is something I would love to have seen, to put alongside northern lights and the aurora.

Saturday 17 February
Ten years ago today my mother died, at Bordean House (a Sue Ryder Home a few miles outside Petersfield), where she had been resident for a number of years. They telephoned at 11 a.m. to say she was unconscious and unlikely to live for more than two hours. I went straight to Bordean and stayed in her room for an hour or so, after which they advised me to go home for lunch and return at two in the afternoon, which I did. While I was sitting there, listening to the rasp of her stertorous breathing, a tall nurse appeared and cheerfully asked if I'd like a cup of tea. I declined. A few minutes later she reappeared, obviously hoping for a death-bed chat. 'You were an only child, weren't you? Did that mean you were a lonely little boy? Did you long for brothers and sisters?' It was kindly meant, I know, but it was profoundly irritating and I snapped. 'All I long for now,' I said, 'is to be left alone with my dying mother.' She withdrew, hurt and haughty. Oh, dear! How I regret myself so often. I came back to the house for a breather; as I entered the door they telephoned to say my poor, very old, rather unhappy mother had died. I returned to Bordean to see her and kiss her farewell. Then it was to the registrar with death certificate and

to the funeral parlour to make the necessary arrangements.

It was dusk when I got to the little funeral shop and the young undertaker, who was expecting me, had kindly hung on for my arrival but, quite visibly, was anxious to finish his day; from the waist down he was in blue-jeans and white sneakers and above desk height in formal black. In offering his condolences he only half-rose from his desk, hoping I wouldn't spot his nether garments.

'Nothing to worry about,' he assured me sympathetically. 'We'll get Mother home in no time!'

'No, no!' I heard myself gasp. 'I have a house-guest!'

The young man informed me he only meant home to the funeral shop. The guest we had was Peggy Ashcroft, who had come down for a long relaxing weekend. She was, as always, marvellous, and absolutely the right person to have around. We downed rather a lot of whisky that night.

I should have visited her grave today but it slipped my mind until awkwardly late.

Spent quite a time thumbing through Michelin, Gault Millau and other guidebooks, speculating about a suitable place for a week's holiday in mid-April.

In the evening played CD of Khachaturian's 2nd Symphony, a rousing piece which suited

145

the cold, rising wind buffeting the house and whining around the doors.

Monday 19 February
The wind in the night ripped off a lot of small branches from the gloomy macrocarpa hedge which runs along a third of our driveway on one side. I have never liked it and I am told it is unlikely to survive more than a dozen years. It was in place when we bought the land forty-odd years ago; with the exception of a fine Atlantic cedar (partially destroyed in the hurricane of 1987) and a couple of cypress trees, all four hundred other trees were planted by ourselves; most of them, it has turned out, too close together. It would be a big hassle to have the macrocarpa rooted out and replaced by something we would never see reach maturity.

The pond is covered at one end with twigs and dead stuff, a couple of garden chairs have been tossed twenty yards from their usual position and a bonsai tree de-potted. Surprisingly a number of tits have appeared at the bird table today.

This morning Matthew telephoned, having just got back from his skiing holiday in Bulgaria. He seems to have enjoyed it but found the meals fairly grim. He said his chalet was pleasant enough but he was puzzled by the showerbath, the floor of which was slanted so that water didn't go down the plug but sloshed into the bathroom. It sounds to me as if the Bulgarians have picked up a few tips from the Spanish. Tony Quayle and I, when filming *Lawrence of Arabia*, rented a wretched little gimcrack house in Almeria for a few weeks. The only way of making the shower work was to sit on the loo, and the only chance of flushing the loo was to turn on the hot tap in the shower. The view from the front of the house was of mangy dogs rutting on a rubbish dump. I am told Almeria has greatly improved in recent years but I'm not going back.

The morning brought joyful news of everything turning out right for a friend who has been in great distress for a long time. 'Loving-kindness in the morning' indeed and an answer to prayers which looked as if they would never be answered.

The evening provided a highly enjoyable dinner (well-shot pheasant and glorious apple tart) at the Parkers', who have just returned from a well-observed, interesting and exotic holiday in South Africa. Merula couldn't be with us as she was feeling a bit low and virus laden. The Parkers had an old friend staying and, somewhat surprisingly for that particular household, much of the talk was of faith-healing; and faith-healing by telephone what's more. I was driven home through whirling snow. The wind dropped and all was silent as I locked up. The snow is about an inch thick and looks very smoothed out. Bright stars.

Wednesday 21 February
Ash Wednesday. Got smudged with ash at St Lawrence at 10 a.m. A full house. All sorts and conditions of us, of every age, returning from the altar marked for death—and life, of course. A salutary experience. I must admit I am always quite happy to see the more sentimental statues covered in their Lenten violet.

This evening we played a CD of Messiaen's *Turangalîla-symphonie.* I often rather like the sounds that Messiaen makes but to my uneducated ear this particular work suggested an orchestra tuning up in a half-hearted way.

Sat down to cauliflower cheese and hope not to have nightmares.

Thursday 22 February
Slight snow in the night but an easy drive up to town, arriving at midday. Lunch with Mu, and then to New Cavendish Street to have impressions taken of the inside of my ears. I was shown a sample of the tiny instrument I shall be wearing; it looked remarkably like that minute snail which is causing such a furore among environmentalists and the bypass builders at Newbury. My little snails are going to cost me nearly £2000. Why should I care *now*, but I'm told that my hearing on low register is as good as that of a boy of seventeen. Very chuffed by the idea. When it comes to the higher frequencies it is, needless to say, total rubbish.

Mark Kingston dined with me at Daphne's in Draycott Avenue. It is totally different from what it was in 1963 when Daphne Rye started it. Daphne had been casting director to H. M. Tennent's; she was round, fleshy and attractive, with a rich, ribald laugh; knew everyone in the theatre world and was a marvellous hostess at the very jolly parties she gave at her house. When it was known that she was seeking capital to start a restaurant dozens of actors, including myself, were on hand to contribute very modest sums by way of investment. It proved a flourishing concern and after ten years, when she sold it and set herself up in Majorca, we all got our money back—but not a penny more. No one grudged her the profit; she had been warm-hearted and helpful in all our lives. It's a swanky place now; good to look at (which it hadn't been), with excellent service and food, but the decibel count was too high for my complete enjoyment. When we left I was first of all handed Barry Humphries's wide-brimmed dark blue or black fedora, then a spiky titfer with leather thongs dangling from a green band; but there was not a sign of my own hat. Profuse apologies as I stumped off baldly and sulkily into a chilly night. I wanted my *own* hat.

Daphne has just telephoned me—I am sitting in my hotel bed scribbling this—it's about 11.30—to say my hat has been traced to

Haslemere and every effort will be made to get it to me tomorrow or Saturday.

Friday 23 February
First to Locke's in St James's Street to get something to wear on my head, which set me back £97. I feared the Haslemere hat fancier might let me down. Then to my doctor who seemed to think my own diagnosis of a possible arthritic hip unlikely. Prescribed a pill. The usual blood test taken. I have never quite trusted blood tests since I had one, about eight years ago, which indicated I had almost every malady known to man and a very short time to live. I knew it was balderdash and insisted I should have another straight away, diagnosed by a different firm. The upshot, a totally clean bill of health. Presumably there was a mix-up and some poor sod, who had got my original one, was reassured he was OK and probably died within a month.

Back at the hotel the concierge handed me—lo and behold—a plastic bag containing my old hat and a bottle of champagne, a kind gift from Daphne's. From now on I shall vigorously deny that the noise level is too high there.

Tonight I took myself to the Young Vic to see *The Misanthrope*, a modernized version by Martin Crimp, directed by Lindsay Posner. Enjoyed it greatly. Sharp, funny and touching. The last fifteen minutes provides an admirable

150

coup de théâtre when the entire cast, with the exception of Alceste (played by the striking Ken Stott), having abandoned their rather drab contemporary clothes, suddenly appear in red Louis XIV costumes and great wigs. Elizabeth McGovern is breathtakingly beautiful in a sort of Inigo Jones fantasy get-up. She and Richard O'Callaghan were the only two members of the cast I knew personally. The acting was impeccable and I loved them all, but I'm sure William Osborne, in particular, has a promising future. There is an amusing 'street-wise' look in his face and movement which will make its mark before long: has probably done so already. Went round to see Elizabeth; we had been together in a film in New York called *Love Sick*, which starred Dudley Moore. I never saw it. We were also together in a TV production here of Christopher Hampton's *Tales from Hollywood*. I was terribly touched that all the cast (I think) came to say Hello when I was chatting with her. The evening was thoroughly worth while anyway but that gesture crowned it for me.

Monday 26 February
I was wrong last week about the snowdrops making a poor showing this year. In the last two days they have put in tardy, rather scattered appearances; far from spectacular but a happy reassurance that spring will come.

A suicide bomb in Jerusalem has killed twenty-five people. Here the IRA has indicated that it is to step up its terrorist attacks and no warnings are to be given. The contempt one feels outstrips any apprehension. In Dublin, Belfast, New York and London yesterday there were massive peace rallies, which is a comfort.

Japheth (labrador type) escaped sometime after nine last night and went courting a neighbour's King Charles spaniel bitch. He kept up his serenading until he was brought back at midnight. Apologies from us this morning, of course. How to make amends? If I send flowers the spaniel may think they are from him. In any case it would be a most unsuitable marriage.

There is a photograph in the paper of a flock of alpaca being reared near Pulborough. They look lovely and not as daunting as llamas. I want one for my birthday but I fear the idea will be frowned on. Only as a pet, of course, and perhaps as a pullover.

Tuesday 27 February
Last night we listened to three Haydn symphonies, something which always gives a sense of well-being and sanity, before switching on the TV to hear how Parliament was dealing with the Scott Report imbroglio. The Government survived by one vote. The House was absolutely full and stormy. Madam

Speaker, that wonderful, intrepid lady, looked as if she was at the wheel of a pirate ship in a high wind, turning vigorously from port to starboard while shouting out her 'Order! Order!' She succeeded in the prevention of foundering.

The tele-box then led us into the calm waters of the House of Lords, where Scott was still the subject. Some of their lordships had their eyes closed and I assumed them to be asleep until old mottled hands began to fumble with hearing-aids when Lady Thatcher rose to speak. I can't think why anyone in this country wants to get rid of the Upper House. They are amusing to look at and sensible, and they manage to discuss issues without shouting or finger-pointing; and the hereditary peers contain, in their own ranks, experts on a great variety of matters. Also they have the immense advantage of not being responsible to any constituencies. Far better to diminish the House of Commons than constitutionally to damage the Lords. Of course it should be occupied only through inheritance and not topped up with temporary titles.

A letter from my doctor to say that the blood test he did last week was fine; no cancer of the prostate. My astonishment when he mentioned the possibility of such a thing, however remote, was profound. So a good bright day followed, full of cobalt-blue sky and white clouds.

Victoria Price telephoned. She is writing a

biography of her father, Vincent, and wanted to quiz me about him and Coral Browne, whom he married. I have never met Miss Price but judging from our talk I bet she makes a good job of the book. Vinney and I had dozens of meals together, either here or in LA or New York but, although I was charmed by him and liked him enormously, I never felt I knew him intimately. Coral was a close friend. We corresponded regularly, at length and with affection. Shortly before she died she sent back all (well, not quite all as it turns out) the letters I had written her. It was a surprise that she had kept any. 'I'm sending them back,' she wrote, 'for you to do what you want with. What we *don't* want is for Alan Bennett to get hold of them and knock them up into a play.' (She was very fond of Alan.) I burned them instantly and Victoria Price has promised to do the same with those which are still around.

Coral's Australian cadence, which often surfaced, always added a witty harshness to her comments on people and life. She sometimes sounded destructive but in fact she was wonderfully kind and generous in every way; it was just that she couldn't resist raising a laugh with her use of words—which were, for the most part, unprintable. There are almost too many stories about her but one I particularly cherish because I witnessed it. Tony Guthrie directed a production of *Tamburlaine* in New York starring her and Tony Quayle. Guthrie invited me to the first dress rehearsal. Coral came on stage before the performance to query some minor point. As always, she looked magnificent and was gloriously dressed in some barbaric style, but perhaps there was a tidge too much hair in her wig. Tony G called out from the stalls, 'Coral, are you happy with that wig?' She stared out front and then said, 'If you really f—ing want to know, I feel as if I'm looking out of a yak's asshole.'

During recent weeks I have been reading a chapter from Isaiah when I have gone to bed. (Don't get me wrong—I am far from holy, as must be apparent, and certainly not holier than thou.) I have no idea what most of it means but throughout Isaiah are scattered odd, wonderful, poetic images. Last night I seized on, 'Behold, I have graven thee on the palms of my hands.' It has intrigued me all day and brought to mind a remarkable early Hindu painting of the soles of the Lord Krishna's feet—bright blue, jolly, rather babyish, with— what?—something circular?—engraved in the centre of each foot. I have a copy of it somewhere but it eludes me.

Have just returned from taking Japheth and Dido for their pre-bed walk; Japheth reluctantly on a lead, because of his amorous intent, and Dido yelping off in a different direction, disturbing all living creatures in the area. A rich glowing moon, brilliant stars and, I guess, a heavy frost about to form. The daffodil shoots all looked like sinister black spikes. Dido came back triumphantly waving a stick which was really too heavy for her. Not a willow; but then she was wafting no love to return.

Wednesday 28 February
Spent half an hour clearing leaves off the surface of the pond; gave up, exhausted with stooping and wielding an inadequate net, with only a third done. It was a lovely fresh afternoon with a cloudless sky; but noise from the A3 spoilt the atmosphere. A beautiful mistle thrush ignored me and the roar of traffic.

My life is feeling poisoned by the knowledge that next Wednesday I have to go to Brighton, attend a book conference and make a short speech. My mind is a total blank as to what I should say and it is likely to stay blank. However, the week after, M and I, joined by Marriott White, are going to escape to Dorset for three nights and I shall be able to hang my head with shame over the River Frome, which I trust will restore me in some way.

I can't have been to that part of the world for nearly forty years. Hardy country and my mother's landscape, though I doubt if she noticed it. The view from an inglenook in a pub was more in her line. Her appreciation of nature and Eng. Lit. was confined to 'Dancing Daffodils' and the novels of Warwick Deeping.

Sorrel and Son was her favourite and I expect she read me in to the character of the son at his posh school.

This evening the Princess of Wales has announced she is prepared to accept divorce. The signals coming from Kensington Palace and Buckingham Palace sound confusing. No plume of white smoke or even black from the chimneys, just a fuzzy grey in fits and starts. It won't disturb my sleep.

What may keep me awake is Updike's *In the Beauty of the Lilies*, which I find hard to put down. Much of it is densely written and sometimes, perhaps, over-detailed; and yet it is often his minute observations that take one's breath away. It seems to me he always sees the truth of things and expresses that truth brilliantly. Can there be another novelist of equal stature writing English today?

Thursday 29 February
Thinking back on *The Misanthrope* at the Young Vic, which I saw a week ago, I feel I should go on record about how witty and funny I thought Niall Buggy as the drama critic, Covington. That name nearly strikes a familiar chord—it combines the names of two London theatre critics. I think of the whole cast with pleasure.

Valerie and Jack Profumo have been on the buzzer to confirm travel arrangements for the four of us in late May. Dame Drue Heinz has invited us for a week to her villa on Lake Como, something Merula and I greatly looked forward to last autumn but which we had to cry off because dates clashed with unexpected work for me: I found myself in Forte's Posthouse hotel near Cambridge instead of a palatial lakeside villa.

We have been to various Italian lakes for holidays but only once managed a day on Lake Como. That was in February 1939. The Old Vic Company, of which I was a member, was doing a tour of Portugal, Italy, Egypt, Greece and Malta. In Milan an English couple kindly offered to take a few of us out to Como. Although it was bitterly cold in Milan we set off in an open car but all was warm and serene when we arrived. Merula and I had married in June 1938 so the Vic tour was like a second honeymoon. Merula had given me as a wedding present a very pricey Leica camera of which I was hugely proud. Somehow it fell in the lake, glug-glug to the bottom. Well, that's *my* memory but M has a different recollection. *She* thinks it fell off a rock in Capri, which I am sure is nonsense; she is thinking of her Box Brownie.

Oh, if only we had written everything down daily we could bore the pants off everyone all the time with our exactitude. I have kept a strictly personal diary, with brief entries, since 1962. Difficult to verify anything before then.

158

MARCH 1996

Friday 1 March
A query from my agent this morning wanting to know if I would be interested in playing Firs in a film of *The Cherry Orchard* in Germany, starting in August. Where, though, do you find cherry blossom at that time of year? I've always been attracted to the idea of playing Firs in the theatre; I'm not so sure about on film. (You need, I think, to see the *whole* man whenever he is about, not close-ups or medium shots or chopped up in any way.) The late Lindsay Anderson invited me to play the part in a film he expected to make in Russia but I dithered—I think I *would* have played it—and eventually the project fell through. That particular film was geared, quite rightly, to cherry blossom time.

The best Firs I have seen was the Russian actor Alexei Gribov who was in the Moscow Arts Company when it came to London in the early fifties. He was a great actor, played three parts here and made a critical success in all of them. When interviewed by the press he gave a classic reply to the perennial question, 'Which is your favourite of the parts you play?' Gribov replied, *sotto voce*, 'I can't tell you that because, you see, it would make the other parts jealous.' A very true observation.

The trousers he wore as Firs were memorable; black, worn, crumpled around the ankles as if he had once been a taller man with longer legs, but it was the drooping trouser seat which was so touching. His back view was a joy. He never cheated or gave any suggestion of self-satisfaction or theatrical cunning. His eyes were always devotedly focused on Madame Ranevsky; he was querulous towards her brother, whom he treated as a wayward child, and his disapproval of the other servants was withering. Another marvellous Firs—which we didn't get to see in performance, only (for those of us in the production) in rehearsal, was Cyril Cusack. Cyril must have been in his late twenties. At the end of the third week of rehearsal war was declared and the company dispersed.

So now I await a script and must decide what I feel about it, speculating whether at eighty-two I'd be capable of acting an eighty-year-old. Actors past fifty are unlikely to have the energy to play King Lear in his dotage satisfactorily.

This afternoon to the Durleighmarsh Farm shop a couple of miles away on the Midhurst road; one of those admirable places where, in season, you can screw off your own squeaky Brussels sprouts, pick your raspberries or beans, etc. They are always fresh and good. The whole atmosphere is a lovely, earthy change from the shiny, dehumanized shelves of the great supermarkets with their 'sell by' dates.

Saturday 2 March
The National Film Theatre's useful little monthly magazine arrived. Looking through it something struck me—the number of photographs of people pointing guns: eleven, to be exact. I'm not quite sure what that says but whatever it is I suspect I don't like it. It won't be long before the wielding of CS gas canisters will be used to grab our attention.

A drab day, most of which was spent coping with correspondence. There are friends whom I have neglected badly during the past several weeks. No good excuse, except that it is lowering to be continually writing of M's hip replacement and its slow progress or all about my eye and Betty Martin.

In the evening we watched an excellent TV interview with Dame Muriel Spark. She came over as wonderfully direct, honest, witty and charming. When she lived in Rome some years ago she invited us to drinks in her splendid apartment. At that time she wore her hair piled high; there were flashing jewels and chic clothes, and she was most affable. The last time I saw her was in June 1991, at the memorial service for Graham Greene. We sat next to each other; we were both required to get up and speak. She wore no make-up and was almost casually dressed. In her tribute to Graham she spoke of the financial help he gave her when she was a struggling writer. She said, 'It was typical of Graham that with the monthly cheques he often sent a few bottles of red wine to "take the edge off cold charity".' It says something very pleasing about both of them.

Very early to bed as M feeling low and feeble. I pray it's not this recurring cold that is going the rounds.

Monday 4 March
Gloomy weather. A surprisingly quick run up to town for a Monday morning. Crowds of tourists pressed to the rails at Buckingham Palace—good pickings for pickpockets or sexual exploration among strangers—but nothing for them to see. The Royal Standard not flying so Ma'am not at home and the military band was already drumming its way towards Hyde Park Corner. A few furled umbrellas were held aloft by raincoated shepherdesses, in an effort to hold their bored-looking flocks together before leading them to pastures new.

Got my hearing-aids (for both outstanding ears) in the afternoon. They have minute antennae, or so I supposed them to be, as if belonging to dwarf Martians, but they are really little lavatory chains to pull the things out. At the moment everything sounds brittle and metallic but I'm told I'll get used to that. To myself I sound like the Ghost of Hamlet senior doing his 'old mole' work in some vault.

Tripped and fell heavily in Jermyn Street. Three kind men converged from different directions as I sat, a bit dazed, in the gutter and helped me to my feet with great concern. As usual, when having made a fool of myself, I was over-apologetic and too effusive with my thanks. There *are* good people around in the streets as well as the muggers. Back to the Connaught feeling bruised. Applied miraculous arnica cream to various places.

To dinner with John and Teresa Wells at their flat. A marvellous, easy evening. Other guests were Frances Partridge, who is keeping pace with the century and will lead us buoyantly and amusingly into the millennium, and Lord and Lady Gibson. We were given the best fish pie ever; I had no idea fish pie could be like that. The red wine, a lovely Pauillac, went admirably with the fish. If only I hadn't talked so much. Also, I should have worn my new contraptions, as I missed quite a lot. Mrs Partridge is not only a total delight but possesses a prodigious, enviable memory. John as witty as ever.

Wednesday 6 March
David Pike drove me to Brighton and back. We left at 10.30 and were at the Grand Hotel by 11.50. This was for a gathering of Penguin Book reps, something which I was dreading but it turned out to be enjoyable. A grey day,

but the sun blazed for an hour on a smooth, dazzling sea; then all returned to pale melancholy. I made a sort of speech which went on too long and left after lunch.

Memories of Brighton crowded in on me as we drove home, from visits as a schoolboy to appearances at the Theatre Royal in later life; from doing the officer training course (for RNVR) at HMS *King Alfred* at the far edge of Hove (it now looks like some sort of leisure complex) to weekends during the fifties at the Royal Crescent Hotel at the eastern end of Brighton front. The town is much given up to the word 'royal'. The Crescent was favoured by a lot of actors on tour when they could more or less afford it. It was run by a Mr and Mrs Taunt, who enjoyed not only the bracing sea air but also a strong pick-me-up soon after breakfast. The pick-me-ups were required pretty frequently until midnight. It was all most friendly and cosy and some of the bedroom suites (very chintzy) had busy little coal fires burning. If the world didn't exactly seem to be my oyster at that time it looked at least promising, and Brighton always provided a rich showing of eccentrics to wonder at.

One of my favourite sights, often seen in the morning, was a tall lady sedately walking the upper promenade with a proprietary air, as if Brighton belonged to her. At a distance one thought, 'What an extraordinary and rather eye-catching fur coat.' By the time one could catch the detail it turned out to be a long coat of roughly stitched pink medicated wool (Thermogene?) with a great rolled collar of ordinary white cotton wool. She was a star in her own right, but intended for long shot rather than close-up. She could have been a name in the silent era of movies.

Also near the Royal Crescent lived dear Douggie Byng, immaculately suited but sporting a wild fur hat and a flowing mauve silk scarf. Larry Olivier and Bobby Flemyng lived within a pebble's throw but *they* were not eccentric.

The Theatre Royal, a handsome theatre, was a pleasure to work in and used a great deal, as it still is, for pre-London presentation; the response of Brighton audiences was supposed to give a good indication of how a play would be received when it reached the West End. I'm not sure that was always accurate. Theatrically it had the disadvantage that it was easy for theatre gossips to slip down from London for a midweek matinée and spread the bad news. T. S. Eliot's *The Cocktail Party* played there prior to opening in New York. I remember us playing one evening to an office party of bewildered typists—it was just before Christmas—and I don't think business was very good throughout the week. In New York the play was received rapturously and had 'House Full' boards outside the theatre for eighteen months. When Tony Quayle and I appeared at the Theatre Royal in Arthur Miller's so-so play about the Holocaust, *Incident at Vichy*, I received an anonymous p.c. from a resident of a house or hotel called 'Heidelberg'. It simply read, 'Who cares about Jews being burned?' No comment necessary, I think. But *there* was one member of the audience who accurately gauged the immediate future of the play. Business at the Phoenix, when the production transferred to London, was poor.

What I liked most about Brighton as a boy was the little electric railway which ran from near the Palace Pier to Black Rock and had a section of its line, all too short for my money, running out over the sea. When the sea was a bit rough this was a thrill; when it was really rough the cissy little train didn't function. I must have spent many happy, if lonely, hours to'ing and fro'ing. Not absolutely lonely. I have always found the sea, in whatever mood it was in, good and sufficient company.

When I got home I had a short rest and then inserted the hearing-aids (rather a tiresome process, I find, although taking them out is easy) and put on a CD of Mozart violin sonatas. I had no idea Mozart could be so shrill. It wasn't uncomfortable or unpleasant, just surprising. Water from taps in a hand-basin had something in common with Niagara, tearing a piece of paper suggested being struck by lightning and the sound of my feet walking across the wooden floor of our living-room was as brash and insistent as flamenco dancing. What a lot I have been missing during the past two or three years. It's all quite refreshing. I am pretty sure sound isn't actually like what I now hear, but what I hear is amusingly new and I think I can live with it.

Thursday 7 March
An invitation from Barry Humphries to lunch one day soon. He writes, 'This is an Australian invitation, that is to say, it is *meant*.' When we briefly encountered two weeks ago, at Daphne's restaurant, I told him how much I had enjoyed his novel, *Women in the Background*. In his letter he says, 'I have just started a kind of sequel called "Dancing Backwards"—which is what women do, as you possibly know.' A very funny and clever man. I look forward to the lunch and his backward dancing. He also says, referring to my memoirs, *Blessings in Disguise*, 'I wish I could say as you do in your last sentence, that I had never lost a friend.' Well, I am adding a few words to that in the reissue of the book later this year. It will now read, after 'Of one thing I can boast; I am unaware of ever having lost a friend,' the words, 'Re-reading that last sentence in 1996, eleven years after it was written, I am saddened to say I can no longer make such a boast. *Mea culpa. Mea culpa. Mea maxima culpa.*'

Jill Balcon and Keith Baxter are coming to dinner tonight. As an experiment I shall stick those little snails in my ears to see how they stand up to overlapping talk. Both guests have good easy-to-listen-to voices and perfect diction. Jill's vocal quality is outstanding; Keith's is rich and doesn't lack volume. Merula is likely to chip in only to kill the point of any story I may embark on. I think she does it when she senses I am getting too loquacious; I *should* be grateful. One gambit is to say to me, very sweetly, 'Tell them about the time when—,' and gives the whole game away in half a dozen words.

There is no grand wine in the house to offer with the veal we are to have but I think a fairly dry, fresh white, with at least a geographical interest, will be 'acceptable'. It is a Chardonnay called Yarden and comes from a vineyard on the Golan Heights.

A huge parcel arrived from USA today. I eyed it with foreboding, suspecting it might contain an assortment of unwanted *Star Wars* plastic toys and figurines. Then I spotted it came from Missouri, from an occasional correspondent whom I have never met or spoken to. I undid the box and inside, after layer on layer of wrapping—I was reminded of those Russian dolls which have other dolls inside them—I came across two finely carved book-ends, made of a variety of beautiful woods; each of them contained a small, secret drawer. The theme of the carving has been inspired by a remarkable passage, a great favourite of mine, in Julian of Norwich's *Revelations of Divine Love* in which she refers to a hazelnut. She speaks of a mental vision in which she saw.

> a little thing, the quantity of a hazelnut, in the palm of my hand, and it was as round as a ball. I thought, 'What may this be?' And it was answered me, 'It is all that is made.' I marvelled how it might last and not fall to nothing for littleness. I was answered, 'It lasts, and ever shall last, for God loves it.'

Then she expiates wonderfully on this image. It is something that has always cheered me; the kind American donor knew that.

The hazelnuts on the book-ends are beautifully done, but I note American hazelnuts must be about three times the size of our native variety. Through many years as an actor I always kept a hazelnut in my make-up box and it was the first thing to be laid out on my dressing-table when I came in to the theatre.

Eliot quoted Julian of Norwich in 'Little Gidding'—

> And all shall be well and
> All manner of thing shall be well.

I think it must have been when reading *The*

Four Quartets that I first came across her. Anyway, she makes some sort of rope or lifeline from the late fourteenth century right up to today.

Saturday 9 March
Yesterday was miserably grey, cold and drizzly. At one time something came out of the cloud and hit one in the face, which felt like frozen millet or canary seed. It didn't qualify as hail. This morning was misty until eleven; then the sun crept through, warmed things up and revealed an unexpected, joyful dash of snowdrops clustered round our sulky, neglected damson tree. Near by there were some dwarf daffodils. Life felt good but the fish knew better; they huddled at the bottom of the pond, hardly moving. Two hours later cold and drabness had returned. When I walked by the pond again I thought I got a 'Told you so!' look from fishy eyes.

Three appeals today from different cancer-relief charities, one OXFAM demand in duplicate, one asking for aid for the mentally disadvantaged and one from USA suggesting I might like to make a contribution to the building of a new recreation room at a Jewish community centre. Also, of course, the weekly offers to double-glaze me. I already see out of a glass darkly.

Still rather creaky from my fall in Jermyn Street last week. Had a masseur over this afternoon to put me to rights; subsequently fell heavily asleep for well over an hour.

In the evening played a CD of Scarlatti pieces. Pretty tinklings, which my hearing jobs picked up well, but wearisome after twenty minutes. Happier with my Updike at the fireside.

Monday 11 March
We arrived in the centre of Wareham at 15.45, David Pike driving my car. It's a pretty little town, architecturally of various periods but, for the most part, gives an impression of red brick and white paint. This is where we shall be, together with Marriott White, for three nights. Weather doesn't look or feel promising.

In the middle of what I take to be the high street (North Street), I asked a personable young lady, 'Can you please direct us to the Priory Hotel, Church Green?' 'Yes,' she said confidently, 'you go back that way and ... No, wait a minute ... No, I don't know. Ask that gentleman coming along. He'll know.' I can't think why she thought so. She faded into the mistiness with a Cheshire Cat smile. I waylaid the advancing gentleman and put the same question. 'Ah, the Priory! You can just about see it from here. The church, that is. Turn left at the next crossing, no the one after that, no it must be the next crossing and keep straight on, wriggling to the right.' I thanked him profusely. Wriggling to the right brought us to

171

a dead end. Some workmen were digging round a barrier across a narrow road. 'Can you direct us, please—etc., etc.' 'Nah.' (or maybe it was 'Nay,' as we are more or less in Hardy country). 'Priory? Never heard of it. You can't get down this way—road's up.' We backed off and within a hundred yards M and David simultaneously spotted the hotel, exactly where you'd expect it to be, alongside the church.

We have a ground-floor suite in the Boathouse, about seventy yards of uneven paving from the main building of the hotel. As its name suggests, it is right on the river (the Frome). The suite is comfortable and warm, perhaps a little dark, but it has French windows which open straight on to a path running alongside the river. The Frome at this point looks as if it's about the width of the length of a cricket pitch. It runs fairly swiftly and appears to be tidal. It probably feeds and is fed by Poole Harbour a few miles away. The hotel grounds are prettily laid out and cared for; in summer they must be very satisfying.

Good bathroom with an alarming Jacuzzi or whirlpool. The bedside lamps, small and pink shaded, are going to prove inadequate for reading in bed; but that is the case in most hotels throughout the world. A Gideon Bible in the drawer in the bedside table doesn't look well-thumbed; in fact it looks as if it has never been opened. Comfortable bed.

Dinner was really excellent; served in the Abbot's Cellar (natch). A pretty, busy, little fire burned in the comfortable, well-decorated hotel sitting-room. All is remarkably quiet; very relaxing. We brought a Travel Scrabble with us but it is too late for intellectual activity. Just time for a couple of very, very silly jokes and then bed.

Tuesday 12 March

Little blue scillas shaking violently in the cold wind, making the borders of garden paths look like running water. The river is quite rough. At home there has been snow. We remained in all morning and then, after a snack lunch, hired a chauffeur-driven car to take us to Corfe, Swanage and the Purbeck Hills. The ruins of Corfe Castle are impressive yet appear skeletal, almost like a cardboard cut-out for a tatty theatre set. Stopped to look at a beautiful little grey village called Worth Matravers, an idyllic spot immaculately kept. When we got out of the car on the top of a hill the bitter, violent wind drove us back inside within five minutes, rubbing our purple noses. But it was good to get a gulp of robust, clean air with a tang of sea on it.

The front at Swanage was closed to traffic (the ubiquitous roadworks) and it was the front I wanted to see again. Somewhere there, overlooking the bay, my maternal grandmother had a whitewashed cottage. Even

173

if it still exists I doubt if I would have been able to identify it; I was about five the only time I was taken to be shown to the old girl. She resembled a vast black widow spider and scared the pants off me. Her great crimson face was surrounded by black hair, fiercely parted in the middle; she was a bundle of shiny black clothes and glittering jet jewellery. Altogether rather gypsy-like, which is surprising, as my mother was auburn haired and freckled. She sat immobile in a large wooden chair in her sitting-room. Years later I heard she had been a heavy boozer. She exuded, as I now see it, something between indifference and dislike, but she gave me what I considered a treasure. Pointing at a small table on which there were a few ornaments she commanded my mother to 'Give the boy the bear.' It was a tiny Polar Bear, about three inches high, covered in white fur and standing on skis. To me it was the most beautiful thing I had ever seen and immediately it became my best friend; well, probably my only friend. I took it to bed with me, helped it slide down pillows; and we exchanged whispered secrets. I can't remember how, in time, I came to lose it. Neither can I recall the name I gave it, but for a long time the little bear lived in my pocket, not with bits of string and marbles but in a clean, comfortable pocket of its own.

After dinner we discussed the idea of Scrabble or me reading something aloud (possibly Eliot's *The Family Reunion*) but decided bed was best.

Don't like any of the news. China is being belligerent towards Taiwan; US aircraft-carrier is heading there; troubled waters. Hong Kong to be faced up to in a year's time. Or, like Suez, will it be before?

Wednesday 13 March
We received a kind invitation to be taken out on the river in a private boat this afternoon, weather permitting. Weather didn't permit; strong easterly wind, little breaking waves on the Frome and the day felt arctic. So that jaunt was postponed for some sunny afternoon in the future. We hired the same car and chauffeur as yesterday and set off for Weymouth, which none of us had ever been to. The sea was driving for the shore with thousands of white horses riding over a pale grey-green surface. Weymouth front we thought pretty; the ironwork balconies on rather flimsy-looking houses suggested New Orleans, if one could imagine New Orleans caked in sea-salt.

Portland Bill was our next objective. The wind there was so strong I had to use all my weight and strength to open the car door. M bravely insisted on getting out too and, with the help of her crutches, struggled a hundred yards but it began to be dangerous, so we abandoned further effort. We were reminded of a cliff-top walk in a gale in the Hebrides a few years ago when the wind forced us to the ground and we had to get back to our car on hands and knees.

From Portland Bill we went on a few miles to see the Cerne Abbas Giant, sprawled in outline on his hillside. He is 180 ft long, they say, and his sexual equipment, in a rigid state, is startling. Our driver told us that women who can't conceive still come to gaze on him, often with successful results. There were two cars drawn up behind ours, each containing youngish to middle-aged ladies. Perhaps it was my imagination that gave them wistful expressions.

Turning on TV News at Ten we were appalled to hear of the ghastly, outrageous shooting of small children in the school at Dunblane, Perthshire. It is a numbing horror and the mind goes blank. Sympathy, comfort, love, tears—no words suffice. M and I went to bed silent and miserable.

Thursday 14 March
Chatting with the owner of the Priory Hotel just before we left and expressing admiration for his beautiful garden, he told us that last year fifty-seven specimen plants had been dug up and stolen by visitors. The flowers and shrubs were chucked over the garden wall, with their name tags attached, and picked up on the other side. I'd love to see some of those petty

thieves name-tagged. One can see the type— hatchet-faced ladies in pleated tweed skirts, well conversant in youth with the Ten Commandments. The same breed who a couple of years ago dug up, at the entrance to our drive, a dozen of our newly planted little American box trees. At £6 or £7 each the thieves did well. I can hear their rasping county voices, 'Stop the car, Phyllis, I can see just what I want! Could it be *Buxus microphylla*?' Then, out with the trowel and trug, but never a prick of conscience. The sort of people who would call the police if they saw a small boy filching one of their apples.

We got home at noon and I gasped with horror when I saw the unwanted mail piled on my desk. I can't think what has been going on to produce this influx. Probably the *Star Wars* films having been issued in video form quite recently account for it. Ah, well—*we* don't have a video.

Friday 15 March
We all mourn bitterly the horror of Dunblane. Mr Major and Mr Blair went up there together to express the national distress and the Queen, they say, will follow. No Moderator, no Archbishop, can give explanation or comfort, however well-intentioned their consoling words.

The gloom spread through a day which, starting cold and dim, managed to provide some hazy sunshine by noon, and the warmth of the afternoon produced little clouds of dizzily whirling midges.

Irene Worth telephoned this evening. She is over here to do her solo performance of Edith Wharton at the Almeida. She says she is exhausted but she sounded very chirpy. She reminded me of our crossing the Atlantic on our way to do *The Cocktail Party* in New York. We used to meet up, very discreetly, in a corner of a vast lounge to quietly rehearse our lines. On one occasion, she says, I suddenly raised my voice to say, 'What had you believed were your relations with this man?' Copies of *The Ocean Times* were lowered in many an armchair and we were stared at. I think we escaped to the promenade deck.

A few sheep are back in the paddock. There is really nothing much for them to eat; moss everywhere. While we ate our tagliatelle supper, eased along with a bottle of Château Cissac, Cru Bourgeois, we listened to Weber's clarinet quintets and felt somewhat restored. Less gloomy, anyway.

Sunday 17 March
Forgiveness. There is going to be a lot said about that today. My experience is that given time—and plenty of it—I can usually bring myself to forgive, quite genuinely, a personal injury, but I find it virtually impossible to forgive an injury to those I love. In fact I don't

know even how to set about it. With age I think you grow alarmingly aware of the trashy heap of unpleasant and unkind things you have said and done during a long life, want to rid yourself of them and to seek forgiveness of others, so it is only right that we should wholeheartedly forgive. But—but, when it comes to the injury done to those we hold dear, I find it all gets more difficult. 'It were better that a millstone were hanged about his neck, and that he was drowned in the depths of the sea.' That refers, of course, to Christ's attitude towards the mental abuse of children, but today everyone's thoughts are turned to the deaths of those sixteen children and the grief of their parents.

It is also Mothering Sunday, the florists' commercial delight—a far cry from the ancient practice of visiting a cathedral or the mother church of the diocese. Before long Father's Day will be upon us—or has it passed?—which used to be the tobacconists' hope.

Yesterday evening I had a long telephone talk with Eileen Atkins. Irene Worth the day before: two Celia Coplestones within twenty-four hours.

After dinner we watched 'Dalziel and Pascoe'. Very good, we thought; excellently directed and beautifully acted. I am, in any case, a fan of Warren Clarke and I have enjoyed Reginald Hill's crime novels.

I was going to jot down, 'The most raw

March in my memory' but the sun came out this afternoon and my blackbird friend looked very relaxed. How do blackbirds remain airborne when only ten inches from the ground? They seem to take huge risks.

At Mass seventeen candles were placed before the altar at St Lawrence and lit by parish children.

Monday 18 March
Should I become a very rich man within the next month (roll on a big Lottery win) I shall turn up at Christie's auction on 19 April and bid for a painting by Joos de Momper and Jan Breugel II called 'A Village Bleaching Ground with Washer-women'. So far I have seen it only in a small reproduction but I am entranced by its unusual subject-matter and its detail. But how did the two artists divide their work? Did one say, 'I'll do the linen spread out on the ground, you do all those people up to various jobs'? Or did they work like our contemporary pair, Gilbert and George, when painting a full frontal attack, each touching up the other's efforts—if that is how it's done?

If the prize isn't big enough to bid for the Momper/Breugel but is still pretty good, I might make an offer for a smallish oil on paper, 'A View of Dovedale' by Sir Thomas Lawrence. It shows a very romantic glade of feathery trees, all lightly done. I shall *not* be bidding for one of those plain white canvases with primary-coloured squares here and there. They usually go for over a million and I feel that, given a good set square, I could knock up something similar myself.

Today I have been a kind of 'twitcher' (an ignorant one) peering through binoculars at a variety of small birds—mostly tits—being very fluttery, aggressive and opinionated round the bird table and nut dispenser. Lots of cases of cage rage and 'anything you can peck I can peck better'.

There are almost universal calls reported in the media for an immediate clampdown on the ownership of small firearms. I cannot understand why the government shilly-shallies about it all, indicating it will take several months to draw up and implement any legislation. If we were suddenly at war action would be swift enough (I hope) and, in a sort of way, this *is* war—against madness, terrorism, fanaticism and sheer wickedness.

During dinner we played a CD of Nielsen's Clarinet Concerto, which lifted our spirits no end.

Wednesday 20 March
Southern Water cut off our supply yesterday from 08.30 until 17.00, as a new pipe is being laid across an adjacent field. At least it's not the Yorkshire Experience, but when we turned on taps in the evening what came gushing out looked like rich tomato juice; a slug of vodka

and a glass of it could have been passed off as a Bloody Mary.

To London this morning. A day for name-dropping; lunch to Dame Drue Heinz at the Connaught and then, at three, we were at St Martin-in-the-Fields for the memorial service for Stephen Spender. Nearly all memorial services these days are called a thanksgiving for the life and work of whoever it may be—sometimes the life has been of doubtful merit and the work meretricious—but in this case it was a genuine thanksgiving for a good man and fine poet.

The church was full and Drue and I were obliged to sit in the front row right under the pulpit. Musically the afternoon was a delight (the Sorrell Quartet playing Haydn, Beethoven and Mozart, and Emma Kirkby singing) and the address, by Professor Wollheim, was the best I have ever heard. Harold Pinter, Matthew Spender, Ted Hughes, James Fenton, Jill Balcon and Barry Humphries all read excellently. There were many public faces to be spotted as Drue and I banged our way down the aisle, Drue knowing them all of course and greeting those within reach. Outside it was drizzling. I didn't think I could face up to the reception being given at the Garrick Club so returned to the hotel.

John and Teresa Wells gave a dinner party at their flat for Natasha Spender. Natasha looked tired—understandably—but upright and resilient. I was very happy to meet Ferdinand Mount (whose *Umbrella* I had recently read) and his wife, and to be able to chat with Barry Humphries—mostly about the Australian painter Conder. I had intended to give him, when we meet for lunch next Wednesday, John Rothenstein's biography of Conder but guessing he might have a copy I telephoned his secretary to inquire; I was more than right; he has two.

All day I have been creaky and have never let my walking-stick out of sight. Only about four months ago a taxi-driver said to me, 'You look chipper for your age, squire. Not even a stick.' Deterioration can be very fast, it seems.

Friday 22 March
Yesterday morning I did a swift household shopping round, gathering goodies for a very small dinner party we are giving tonight. Went to Charles in Elizabeth Street to pick up smoked salmon, to Roux in Ebury Street for an exotic pudding (plus a *boudin* which we had last night washed down with a bottle of cider) and to Fry's for asparagus and fruit. From Fry's I could spot the dapper figure of Sir Dirk B as he disappeared towards his home with his bag of healthy veg. On to Pulbrook & Gould for branches of eucalyptus leaves, guelder roses and dazzling ranunculus.

Marriott (musical Marriott White) had sent us a tape, which arrived today, of 'Tenebrae

Responsories' by Victoria (1548–1611, it informs us) sung by the Tallis Scholars. She had warned me I might not care for it. On a first hearing it worked on me like a diuretic. Perhaps I'll get more out of it next time. Or vice versa.

Ron Harwood telephoned me asking if I would be interested in reading a new play he has written. I said I would always be happy to read any play he sent so long as he didn't expect me to act in it. He is wonderfully good-humoured and knew immediately that I wasn't trying to be rude but just saying I'm past it all.

Too wet to go out to feed the fish; they must just swim around until tomorrow.

Saturday 23 March
For my taste the best thing on BBC radio (Ch. 4) is the Shipping Forecast. It is romantic, authoritative, mesmeric and understandable. The girl who speaks it has a good, clear, unaffected voice, and she treats all areas with total impartiality. Today we had, among many excitements, 'Finisterre, intermittent rain, visibility one mile, and rising slowly.' There was no moral judgement in her voice when she added, 'Dover, visibility ten metres, falling rapidly.' I love this tour of the seas around our coasts and the information about what is happening in the Bay of Biscay and in Spanish waters. My imagination provides me with stinging spray and I think I hear breakers and

the clanging bell of a buoy.

A friend in NY has sent me a theatre magazine containing a very eulogistic article on Irene Worth and an interview with her. The praise is well deserved but I was somewhat surprised to see her quoted as saying she had been a *founder* of the Stratford [Ontario] Festival (which opened in 1953), together with Tyrone Guthrie and myself. I certainly wasn't a founder. My recollection is that it was the brainchild of Tom Patterson, a citizen of Stratford, aided by a number of well-heeled local enthusiasts. They approached Guthrie and he contacted me. Half a dozen of us from England were enticed to Canada, including Irene, for virtually no money. In the circumstances that seemed fair enough. Guthrie told me that Irene wanted in her contract a clause which would provide her with a car, chauffeur and lady's maid. When it dawned on her that it was something of an experimental adventure she sportingly settled for a bicycle.

Goodness, that was forty-three years ago and the Stratford Festival is now a firmly established and highly regarded Canadian institution.

Switched on TV to watch 'Dalziel and Pascoe'. Complicated but enjoyable. I couldn't make out why one of the corpses was wearing a wig. I still don't know how to pronounce Dalziel.

Sunday 24 March

The raising of Lazarus from the dead is the subject of today's Gospel. The current sub-supermarket translation has Christ asking, 'Where have you put him?'—as if Lazarus might be a basket, and later, 'Lazarus, here! Come out!'—as if calling a terrier digging in a rabbit warren.

Today is the fortieth anniversary of my 'reconciliation' with the Holy, Roman, Catholic and Apostolic Church. I rejoice in that and wish it had come decades earlier, but vulgarisms such as the above have proved a prickly cross to bear for converts like myself. Latin was far from my strong point at school and yet I miss its sonority in the essential and unchanging parts of the Mass. The poor Anglicans have to put up with similar banalities in their modern versions, which seem to be very similar to *Private Eye*'s 'Rocky Horror Service'.

March 24, 1956, was sunny and hot. Veronica Turleigh (Mrs James Laver), who was one of the two RCs I knew well, came down to Petersfield to support me. I was received at St Lawrence by Fr. Henry Clarke. Fr. Clarke's best known convert was Group-captain Cheshire, vc, whom he had received in 1946. The eventual result of that was the foundation of the Cheshire Homes; a worldwide success and a comfort to thousands.

I ran into him briefly a few times, here in Petersfield, in London and Bangalore. His modesty, simplicity and sheer ordinariness were awe inspiring; he also had a quiet charm. We never got much beyond the annual exchange of Christmas cards but I always felt better for having encountered him. In good time I suppose the process will start which will lead to him being called Blessed; and eventually, I hope, his canonization. That should be a proud day for Petersfield, even if the local paper fails to notice it.

It must have been in the sixties that David Lean, who was friendly with Cheshire, told me of an odd incident he had witnessed in New Delhi. Nehru had invited him and Cheshire to tea at Government House. At the time, Cheshire was desperate to get hold of a poor piece of land in northern India on which to build one of his homes, but foreigners were forbidden to buy or own land. All his requests had been firmly dismissed. David said that during tea Cheshire was consumed with shyness and never spoke a word, although he was very aware he was in the presence of the one man in the world who could help him. When it was time for them to leave Nehru asked Cheshire how he was getting back to his hotel. Speaking for the first time he said he would take a bus or tram and then walk. Nehru ordered his own car, saw Cheshire into it (an almost unheard of courtesy) and stood waving until the car was out of sight. Then, with tears in his eyes, he turned to an aide and said, 'That is the greatest man I have met since Gandhi. Give him the land I know he wants.' Things worked like that so often for Cheshire.

Merula's sister Chattie came for the day and night and an old actor/painter friend of theirs, Ole Pooley, arrived for lunch, so conversation was more or less confined to reminiscences. Ole is a week or two older than me, lives in LA, still plays vigorous tennis, swims a lot, walks a lot and obviously has all his marbles. I felt a bit put out.

The news of the European ban on British beef left us all talking, depressingly, about Mad Cow Disease and its human equivalent. 'When,' I wondered, 'did I hear talk about doubtful beef long ago?' Suddenly it came to me; it was when I was playing Andrew Aguecheek to Larry Olivier's Toby Belch at the Old Vic in 1936.

AGUECHEEK: I am a great eater of beef, and I believe that does harm to my wit.
TOBY: No question.
AGUECHEEK: An I thought that, I'd forswear it.

Wednesday 27 March
A bright chilly day; David Pike drove me to town. Went to the National Gallery to see the Velazquez portrait of Pope Innocent X on loan from the Doria Pamphilj Gallery in Rome. It is

188

much lighter in texture and colour than reproductions had led me to expect. You feel you are in the presence of the man—at least, I did—that you have met him before, are aware of his weaknesses (but wouldn't dare express them) and, of course, of his strength. His right hand is remarkably delicate, almost feminine, which goes oddly with his power. I wouldn't like to stay very long in his company in case he turned nasty. There is, I think, a sadness in his eye as well as wariness; the burden of his pontificate seems to have hunched him. I wanted more time to look but a bevy of dishevelled, dirty-haired, pigeon-toed French students, behaving brashly, made the atmosphere intolerable. As I turned away I was nearly tripped up by a crocodile of five-year-olds, English I think, who steadfastly threaded their way through the rest of us. At least they were silent. In fact they looked peaky and scared. Couldn't see who was in charge of them: some latter-day Miss Jean Brodie, I expect.

On either side of the Velazquez are marble busts of Innocent, each of which is like the portrait but younger and more vigorous. They both bore a remarkable resemblance to the late Harry Andrews. I saw Harry many times contemplating his make-up in a dressing-room mirror and looking just like those busts. Francis Bacon, if I may say so, is not in the Velazquez league. The thought of those young

French students, so much better educated than their British counterparts, continues to irritate me. In my experience they behave just as tiresomely in their own country.

In 1993, on our first visit to the little Burgundian hilltop town of Vézelay, the glorious Romanesque basilica was invaded by a hundred or more French adolescents. Freed from their school buses they charged, screaming and shouting up and down the aisles. Thomas à Becket, Richard Coeur de Lion and Louis VII of France had all climbed to that cathedral; I like to think that if those three had encountered such goings-on they would have had a field day head bashing.

It was similar a year before when we went to Colmar. In the Unterlinden Museum a crowd of adolescents milled about in front of the great Grünewald 'Crucifixion', surreptitiously smoking but quite flagrantly groping and giggling. Well, I must admit the Nat. Gal. tourists were not as awful as that.

To the table-hopping Ivy where Barry Humphries gave me lunch. He had pinched Melvyn Bragg's corner. Enjoyed his company immensely. Nowhere in his nature do I detect Dame Edna. Like most comedians he dresses formally but with a give-away Aussie-type hat. After lunch I scoured Charing Cross Road and the small passageways off it for a copy of the Talmud. No luck. In one shop they hadn't even heard of it.

This evening I took Faith Brook to the Haymarket Theatre to see *An Ideal Husband*. It must be nearly sixty years since I last saw it and I recollected nothing, of plot or cast. The play wears well. Production by Peter Hall; distinguished acting. During the performance a large percentage of the audience sat lapping up their ice-cream with wooden spatulas. (I didn't notice what they did with their empty cartons.) Some of the staff could be heard chattering on the other side of the stalls doors, rather louder than some of the cast. They gave a clear indication of when the curtain was about to fall. It is still a beautiful theatre; haunted I know, but not haunted by the classy elegance it once had.

Friday 29 March
The Oscars have come and gone and I forgot about them in spite of the hype and speculation. I liked Emma Thompson's acceptance speech for her script of *Sense and Sensibility* as reported in the press; and I was delighted that Wallace and Gromit got an Oscar for Mr Park.

I fail to understand all the stuff written about how an Oscar sends an actor's salary soaring. The film company's box-office takings undoubtedly rise but—well, certainly not *this* actor's salary. Two Oscars (one for services to the cinema) have come my astonished way in addition to two nominations. Three years ago I was offered $10,000—call it £7000—to be in New York for a month, at my own expense, to play a part (admittedly small) in the film of *The Age of Innocence*. I declined. At the beginning of the Gulf War I had a Hollywood offer of approximately $20,000 to work over there for sixteen weeks. I told them to forget it. They instantly offered a million. When I said I was no longer interested (although the script had something) and, in any case, none of us knew whether the war in the Gulf would inconveniently escalate, they upped the million by offering me the use of a private jet. The accountants who now seem to manage the deals for the big companies lack tact. I have always resented the idea that every man has his price. Not this old baby.

It has been a bright, invigorating day. The dogs were in bouncing form until someone started rabbit shooting in the late afternoon, which drove Japheth to sitting under the kitchen table and Dido to hiding in the darkness of the downstairs loo.

Mgr Murtagh came up during the evening to discuss Easter Vigil plans and how my reading of the opening verses of the Book of Genesis is to fit in. The lady who conducts the choir wishes to have a little musical contribution between each section of the story of Creation. OK—but I am apprehensive of it all getting a bit long, and I want to know if the choir is going to be standing, sitting or, more worryingly, getting up and down each time they perform. All will be sorted out in a day or two. Mgr Murtagh stayed to share our cauliflower cheese. Conversation was, as usual with him, mostly of Italy and Italian peasants. He is good company, an admirable, patient priest, highly regarded by his parishioners, but I wish he wasn't such a workaholic.

Sunday 31 March
Oh, dear! I hate myself today. At Mass this morning I replied abruptly when a woman sat down beside me and asked, knowingly, if I was who she thought I was. I fear I spoiled Palm Sunday for both of us.

Yesterday was bright but chilly. Alan B turned up in the afternoon and is staying for dinner tonight. In good form. He is the most easy guest, as he always makes his own tea (endlessly) and knows where everything is to be found.

Moved the clocks forward an hour when we went to bed. M, needless to say, anxiously queried whether they shouldn't go *back* an hour; and that in spite of hearing the man on the news clearly state they should go forwards.

At 03.00 I woke with a start, convinced that I heard secret whistles being exchanged in the house. Switching on the light I found Michaelmas the cat sitting on the bedside table, saucer-eyed and making z-z-z noises of pleasure. Carried him downstairs—he kept up his z-z-ing—and shut him in the kitchen. Whenever he has appeared upstairs in the night, having cleverly evaded being put out, he has looked triumphant.

This evening we watched and listened to the finals of the BBC Young Musician of the Year competition; always moving, and always something which makes one try to revalue all the arts.

APRIL 1996

Monday 1 April
The BBC Young Musician of the Year competition last night was won by eighteen-year-old Rafal Payne, who played the Khachaturian Violin Concerto. It was a beautiful performance but I somehow wished the prize to go to Sam Watson for his banging, pinging, tapping and brushing of a battery of percussion instruments. I can't think how he knew where they all were as he darted about in search of something to hit. It was Richard Rodney Bennett's Percussion Concerto. Both young men were modest, unaffected and had charming personalities.

Up to London. Arrived in Chelsea in record time and then we were snarled up for twenty minutes by huge tourist buses, mostly half empty, trying to manoeuvre themselves up St James's Street.

To Tower Records to try to get the Rodney Bennett but the girl with the ring through her lower lip had never heard of him. Her diction was not of the best. Anyway they had no Rodney Bennett.

In the evening took myself to see *Il Postino*. It was moving, funny, adorable and exquisitely acted. It now takes place alongside *My Life as a Dog* and *Strictly Ballroom* as one of my favourite films of the last decade. It had the freshness and ironical wit of the great post-war Italian films.

Tuesday 2 April
Bright and rather chilly. At 13.00 went to the Equity Office at the top of Upper St Martin's Lane to unveil a plaque in celebration of a hundred years of cinema. It has my name on it but I am only eighty-two—today. I pulled a cord which brought down half of its red veiling on my head and the other half on the president of Equity. I couldn't see what was written on the plaque so when a microphone was thrust at me I made an unprepared speech of a few ill-chosen words. Next time I'm in London I shall have a good look at it.

Sixty-two years ago today I made my first professional appearance, at the King's Theatre, Hammersmith—long demolished. The play was *Libel!* put on, directed and acted in by Leon M. Lion, a rather alarming, taciturn, beetle-browed actor/manager. Also in the cast were Nigel Playfair (always delightful), Malcolm Kean and Frances Doble, a Canadian beauty. My humble job was to sit in the jury box wearing a lot of make-up. I think I was paid twelve shillings for the week we were there but this was raised to a pound when we moved to the Playhouse. There was an extremely kind stage-manager, Matthew Forsyth, who gave me two lines to understudy.

When I got home this afternoon I found a vast pile of mail which dismayed me, knowing I shall have to write thank-you notes for much of it. Matthew had come down yesterday and kindly left for me his usual plethora of brilliantly chosen gadgets. This year he provided me with something which recharges ordinary batteries, a Japanese contraption which enhances sound and a 'miracle' watering-can which directs a jet of water wherever you want it to go. *That* is going to prove very useful as Merula has given me a trough of beautiful, variegated hydrangeas.

Thought I might enjoy a TV programme on hurricanes but got bored after ten minutes watching bending palm trees and metal sheets being blown along wet streets in Miami, and listening to the memories of people living in Florida. I have my own vivid memories of a hurricane, waterspouts and frightening storms. Switched off and put on a CD birthday present of Evgeny Kissin playing Schubert, Brahms and Liszt. Am saving for tomorrow another CD present (of Barbirolli conducting the *Dream of Gerontius*) from Bernard Hepton, whom I got to know in the Smiley TVs and haven't seen or been in touch with for years.

Thursday 4 April
I have always been apolitical; except when I was about eighteen and called myself a Communist, without the least knowledge of

Marxism, Leninism or, come to think of it, anything else. It was a short-lived phase encouraged by a friendly ex-schoolmaster. What I particularly liked doing was slipping Communist literature through letter-boxes under the cover of night; this seemed to my innocent mind both dangerous and subversive. For a year or so I was an avid reader of Left Book Club publications, until it dawned on me that the books bored me stiff and my left-wing slant was really all a pretence. If, after that, I inclined any way it was towards the Liberals. Most Liberal attitudes had their appeal but after a while I realized that many of the Liberals I encountered were fearful snobs; very Whiggish. Beloved Trollope was Whiggish, in an even-handed way. This morning, rummaging in a drawer, I found an old notebook, dated 1973, in which I had copied out the following:

'Mrs Proudie considered herself to be in politics a pure Whig; all her family belonged to the Whig party. Now among all ranks of Englishmen and Englishwomen (Mrs Proudie should, I think, be ranked among the former—on the score of her great strength of mind) no one is so hostile to lowly born pretenders to high station as the pure Whig.'

An early-morning frost but the daffodils have remained upright and by Sunday should be in full array. Even *Anemone blanda*, of which there was hardly a glimpse yesterday, are suddenly showing buds. A number of siskins are flitting around and pigeons bowing rapidly to each other.

The Queen has distributed Maundy money in Norwich, but did she touch any citizens for scrofula?

The roar of Easter traffic is on us. I stood and watched the lemmings in their rushing cars, all too close together and doing something in excess of 70 m.p.h. Yesterday there was a very unpleasant pile-up just a mile away.

Haven't managed to catch the comet yet. The moon tonight is startlingly like a blood orange.

Tomorrow night we shall watch 'Eskimo Day'—re-titled from 'Interview Day', but I shall refrain from comment. I know already what I think about my own dismal performance. My admirable fellow-actors can manage quite well without any patronizing accolade from me.

Saturday 6 April
Each week Merula puts on my desk a small vase of flowers she has picked. I rarely see her do this; her loving gestures are nearly always a surprise. This morning's offering is of three minute dwarf daffodils, a few scillas, some balsam poplar leaves and something that looks like Rice Krispies threaded on cotton.

Listened, as we do most Saturday

lunchtimes, to 'Any Questions'. It is usually fairly good entertainment but my spirits drop when those political women start spouting, not so much because of what they say (though God knows that can be irritating), but because I fear their flat-out, breathless, non-stop speechifying is going to last for ever. They also interrupt other speakers and sooner or later (too late, so often) Dimbleby has to call them to order, which he does over-politely.

The passage from Genesis which I am to read tonight at the Easter Vigil I have said aloud to myself five or six times. Where to take breaths is proving a problem and I keep changing my mind. In past years a breath, consciously taken, could carry one firmly through a short sentence, or even a couple of lines of Shakespeare, but with age a breath seems to be called for after very few words. It's a horrible feeling for an actor having to sacrifice his sense of rhythm to accommodate wheezy lungs.

The Jerusalem Bible translation has, 'God said, Let us make man in our own image, in the likeness of *ourselves*.' There is a theological statement in that which appeals, and I expect I shall emphasize it; but I am fearful of being too emphatic with, 'Male and female he created them.' Don't want to offend any extreme 'gay' activists. But not at St Lawrence of course.

Friends saw today a golden oricle a few hundred yards from the house. It's a bird I have never spotted but Merula, who is pretty good at bird identification, says she saw one once in Sussex before we were married—so that is over fifty-eight years ago.

Dusk is falling so I must go to put on my best suit for a scrutinizing congregation. I feel quite nervous, as I always did on first nights in the theatre or when the cameras started rolling on a new film. My comfort will be in witnessing the re-kindling of fire, the lighting of the paschal candle, the blessing of water, the sound of Easter bells and all those ancient reassuring things.

Monday 8 April
The Island Race has been given a bright, sunny but not very warm Bank Holiday which ought to cheer us all up until the next one in four weeks' time. I bet it doesn't. The Easter weekend is always chosen for demonstrations, to hold up fire-engines and ambulances going about their civic duties or to have rowdy conferences in ugly halls. And the May holiday will be probably the same.

Yesterday Piers Haggard and his wife Anna came to lunch. They had been warned that it would be meagre—just kedgeree washed down with Cloudy Bay followed by an apple flan. I hope they got some enjoyment from their visit, as we certainly did. There was a certain amount of talk about 'Eskimo Day', which Piers had directed, reminiscences (from us) about his

201

father, Stephen, and mother, Morna and our distress—indeed anger I suppose—at the mad, unpleasant behaviour Peter Sellers displayed in the last year or so of his life. Our only disagreement lay in our totally opposite assessments of *Il Postino*, which I had loved and the Haggards rather dismissed.

In the evening M and I watched the TV of *Gulliver's Travels*, directed by Charles Sturridge. We found it enormously enjoyable and exciting but were exasperated by the constant interruptions for commercials. I made a vow to avoid for the rest of my life all the products advertised, from fast cars I can't afford, to banks I don't need or shampoos for lovely, silken, flowing hair. The interruptions were particularly unfortunate as the film itself is rather chopped up with flashbacks or flash-forwards, so at times it was rather bitty. Fascinating script and a remarkable technical achievement. The only grumble I have (apart from the aforesaid) is that with all the brilliance of design and trickery we were not given one of the most memorable incidents in Lilliput—Gulliver towing away the enemy fleet. What was substituted for this was imaginative—seeing Gulliver swimming under water to lift the fleet's anchors from the seabed—but not up to the sight we coveted. Three or four years ago John Wells achieved this in a rough and, perhaps, not quite ready workshop production at the National Theatre of his own brilliant stage version. He had a dozen young actors, a couple of stepladders, some white tablecloths and coils of rope, and the fleet came swaying towards us with remarkable life. I have longed for him to tackle it again but I fear that with proper financial support it might get elaborated and so spoiled. What is really wanted is money to keep the actors on a decent wage for a few months, so they can be welded together, and keep the props exactly as they were that summer afternoon in a bare rehearsal room.

Easter Day 1994 was on 3 April, a day after my eightieth birthday, and a day Merula and I are unlikely to forget. We were in Rome for a week, staying at the Hotel Inghilterra (which has come up in the world since the time we used it frequently thirty years ago) and we saw a lot of our friend Fr. Derek Jennings, who died last year. Among various treats Derek managed to arrange for us (ah, the machinations within the powerhouse of the Catholic Church!) was a couple of diplomatic corps tickets for the Pope's Easter Mass, which was to be held outside St Peter's.

That Sunday no Roman augur would have been required to look into the entrails of some wretched bird to inform the Pontiff that the signs were grim. A glance out of our bedroom window at 7 o'clock showed ominous black clouds speeding from the north—'bubbling up' as BBC weather presenters are apt to say—and the wind crashed our unhinged shutters. 'I hope,' I said to M, 'that someone at the Vatican has had the wit to draw the Holy Father's attention to what is in store for all of us and that in his compassion he will give orders to shift the proceedings to inside the basilica.'

We had been advised in stern words to be in our places before 10. The Mass was to start at 10.30. Being over-punctual as well as dutiful we made it past the scrutinizing eyes of the tall, elegant Switzers by 09.45 and were courteously shown to our red plush chairs in the front row, surrounded by ambassadors with their wives in black lace mantillas. As we turned up our raincoat collars against the bitter wind and settled down the heavens opened. Lightning flashed and rain hit us at a penetrating angle. A distinguished gentleman in a Homburg hat, which was already looking like a Bernini fountain, disappeared from my side and returned minutes later with a large broken umbrella which he gallantly presented to Merula. It was I who had to manage it in the wind, of course. By this time we were soaked to the skin and our teeth were chattering. A man in a stiff white bow-tie (celluloid?) and clinging tails and squelchy shoes appeared from a side-door in St Peter's and distributed, to all of us whom he could reach, black plastic bin-liners. It was a kind gesture but far too late. A girl in a cotton frock sitting just behind us succumbed to a rigor. A thousand white, starched coifs, which half an hour before had looked like a great aggressive Armada, went limp and the nuns fell silent without a shot being fired. And then His Holiness appeared.

We all stood and tried, in the Italian fashion, to clap our wet hands. He walked slowly and steadily to the altar under its vast canopy. At the appropriate moment we sat again on our red plush chairs. The sensation was that of sitting in a chilled, sodden summer pudding.

The Mass itself was gravely impressive, celebrated by the Pope at a measured pace, with no flourishes or theatricality. I decided that his voice is the most beautiful and dignified speaking voice I have ever heard; I was within ten yards of him for an hour and feel that my impression was justified. It is also a very powerful voice; something unexpected when you see his rather stooped frame. Shortly before noon he withdrew into the Vatican and we decided we were far too wet to wait for the blessing of the City and the World. The Swiss Guards stood solidly throughout the storm, reminding me of Sir Edward Poynter's 'Faithful unto Death'—the painting of that stalwart Roman soldier, with a grim apprehension in his eye, standing firm while Pompeii succumbed to all that Vesuvius could throw at it by way of burning rocks. That, and the picture of poor Captain Oates setting off from the tent in such unthinkable weather, were the two preferred classroom paintings at my prep school.

M and I got back to our hotel, changed out of our dripping clothes and made our way to the English College where we had been invited to lunch. It proved a very jolly, noisy occasion with, at the end of the meal, dozens of seminarians quite clearly aiming the corks from their Spumanti bottles at their ecclesiastical boss.

Tuesday 9 April
Last night we watched the second part of Gulliver and particularly enjoyed Johnny Gielgud's brief, sunny appearance, mangling cucumbers in the hope of turning them into bottled sunlight. He managed to look rather like a cucumber.

Not having been to the Cézanne exhibition at the Tate we turned on the box again, later in the evening, to be escorted round the gallery by George Melly, Loyd Grossman and Sarah Kent. Didn't get much of a look at the pictures because Melly's vast hat so often occupied most of the screen; also Miss Kent's gestures were distracting rather than illuminating. A pity, as they seemed to have the place to themselves—though of course they always knew where the camera was. I know I am fearfully old fogeyish but I have always liked the good manners of men taking off their hats in elevators and at exhibitions.

This morning was misty and cold. M is feeling off colour and Dido has been sick all day. M had no lunch and only a baked potato for dinner; Dido wouldn't look at anything but half a teaspoonful of whisky and boiled water. The house seems quietly melancholy without Dido's shrieks at squirrels she spies through the window, yet when she does shriek I yell with exasperation.

Wednesday 10 April
A director of social services in Glasgow, a Miss Hartnoll, appears to have made a report in which she claims that the drug Ecstasy is probably less harmful than aspirin. This statement is supported by a medical psychiatrist. The likelihood of death from Ecstasy is negligible, they say. No mention, apparently, of brain damage, which is causing such concern in USA. Brain damage for life, that is: a sort of living death for the victim and permanent deep distress for family and friends. Pass me an aspirin; an aspirin I'm told can help stave off a stroke.

A telephone call from Henrietta Gough to say Micky Gough has sailed through the complicated operation he had on his leg yesterday. Another happy piece of news today has been a card from Ed Herrmann excitedly announcing that his wife has presented him with a baby girl.

After a clouded day a vial of bottled

sunlight, not of the best vintage, has been poured out on the evening air. Dido is back from the vet with a medicine chest bigger than herself; she has been recommended a little sponge cake soaked in weak tea. This has been offered and refused, but a glimpse of a squirrel on a tree has sent her bounding out so I don't think she is too bad.

Merula goes to see her own vet tomorrow.

Thursday 11 April
Dido reluctantly swallowed a small piece of sponge cake, soaked in tea with a touch of glucose; a couple of hours later she decided that what she wanted most in the world was a sliver of chicken, and then more chicken. She had to be restrained after that. So all is going well and our anxiety is evaporating.

Merula has been given some Stemetil pills to help her ward off moments of feeling unbalanced. We have cancelled going to London on Sunday week for the opening of an exhibition of her brother Mikey's paintings. A great relief to me. Soho on a Sunday night, in and out of taxis, standing around making conversation, greeting relations—she is simply not up to that yet. Much better to go to the exhibition in early May. (Mikey died of leukaemia in '87.)

I have a great feeling that the farmer who maintains mad cow disease has been caused by a penetrating chemical sprayed on the animals' spines is right and the government expert wrong. It appears that when he asked for a test to be carried out the officials used a slightly different chemical to the one he had specified, the one which had been prescribed for a number of years by the Minister of Agriculture. I don't give much credence to conspiracy theories in any field but there is, I can't help feeling, a whiff of cover-up in this area.

Israel has launched an air and sea attack on Hezbollah hideouts south of Beirut. Trouble there seems endless and meaningless. I have only been to the Lebanon once, when I managed to snatch a few days' holiday from filming *Lawrence of Arabia* in Jordan. That must have been in 1962. Obviously, things have changed drastically and distressingly since then but even at that date the outskirts of Beirut were rubbly, although from building construction rather than destruction. It seemed to me a rather glamorous place with a very pronounced smell; expensive French perfumes in the shopping areas mingling with spices and the all-pervasive saltiness of the eastern Mediterranean. Sauntering along the front as the sun went down over a calm sea was wonderfully relaxing. And today everyone has to run for cover.

Saturday 13 April
This week's *Spectator* carries an article about

the late Sir Harold Acton and the legal wrangle which has arisen about his estate. His remarkable Renaissance villa, La Pietra, just outside Florence, was left to New York University. His offer of it to Oxford University was, unaccountably, turned down and that hurt him. Now a lady in Florence claims to be Acton's half-sister and wants a share of his goodies. (I am tempted to say, 'Watch this space,' but I imagine it would mean watching for years, litigation being what it is.) In April 1972, when M and I were holidaying in Fiesole, just above Florence, we were kindly invited to a lunch party at La Pietra. Eight of us sat down to table and I was astonished to see the very smart, white-gloved servants hiding behind large painted screens; it might have been a scene from the court of Louis XV. There must have been spyholes in the screens because without any audible or visible sign the servants reappeared to collect or deliver plates at exactly the right moment.

Lunch was a light-hearted gossipy affair. He kept us entertained with a variety of anecdotes, wittily told; astonished us with an account of the minuscule tipping of his servants by royalty and, I think it was on the same occasion, by his tale of the behaviour of a world-famous film star and beauty who had recently come to lunch. (No name, no pack-drill.) He noticed, as he was showing her round the house, that her capacious handbag was open and into it she surreptitiously flicked various bibelots that caught her eye. As she was about to leave, her car at the door, she graciously thanked him for lunch and bestowed a little moue of a kiss. 'And now,' Acton said, in that rather high, fluting, hesitant and humming voice he had, 'and now, er—my dear, shall we go round the house again and—mm—you can put back in their proper places all the—er—pretty little things in your—mm—handbag?' She complied and left silently. Well, better that than having the *carabanieri* round.

Two days after lunch he invited M and me for drinks so we could have a quiet look at his superb pictures and stroll in the glorious gardens.

I didn't know him at all well and cannot remember when I first briefly met him or with whom. When I was playing at the Haymarket in 1972, in John Mortimer's *A Voyage Round my Father*, he came backstage to see me. It so happened that Noël Coward came the same night so I had the two of them sitting opposite each other in my dressing-room—which Acton would probably have called *'ma loge'*—and I sensed that neither was comfortable in the other's company. Acton was tall, Chinese-Mandarin-like with a head and face that looked like polished ivory; Coward, too, was fairly tall and also suggested something oriental in his looks. I sat between them, eyeing them warily as I removed my make-up. Acton smiled his polite Chinese smile. If it was discomfiture he wished to inflict on Coward he succeeded hands down. He kept formally bowing from the waist while he spoke. 'Ah—the, er—mm—the honour—(bow)—the very—er—*great* honour (bow) of being in the presence of the one and only Noël Coward (bow). Known to us all—er—mm—as The Master.' Noël was deeply embarrassed and kept making little deprecating gestures with a finger but was, amazingly, at a loss for words—that is, until Harold Acton had made his exit.

It has been a beautiful sunny day—perhaps not as warm as one could wish for at this time of year, but lifting to the heart all the same. Have played again the CD of Evgeny Kissin doing his Schubert, Liszt and Brahms pieces, which seem to go hand in hand with the weather.

Algae is beginning to form in the pond so the fish look dim when at the bottom. A nuisance; very expensive to deal with.

Monday 15 April
Jeanne Moreau telephoned yesterday morning. That's always a pleasant surprise. She is over here to receive an Academy Fellowship from BAFTA. She is, I think, the most interesting actress I know and I wish to heaven I had had the chance to work with her twenty or more years ago. Our professional lives have crossed only once, in the BBC's 'A

Foreign Field'. All the time I have worked in films I have been painstakingly good at 'hitting my marks' on the studio floor in an effort to satisfy directors and technicians, and I have also made an effort, when repeating a scene, to make it an exact replica of the previous 'take'. Jeanne demonstrated that such exactitude was deadening. Watching her filming I knew she was right; every 'take' was slightly different and every one was spontaneous and fresh. If I had been freed from my self-imposed strait-jacket three decades ago I might—who knows?—I might have taken off and been a sort of star. Not that I ever had any ambition to be a film star; I saw a few actors cease to be real people when they succeeded and some of those who failed become ingrained with bitterness. And some of the good ones who made it to the top didn't know how to cope with their success and reached for the bottle. Updike's *In the Beauty of the Lilies* gives a full-length, devastating portrait of a Hollywoodized human being. No thank you.

Shortly after lunch yesterday there was a thud on a window-pane in the living-room; a female bullfinch had knocked herself out. She was lying on the ground and her husband stood beside her, bewildered. When M went out to pick her up he disappeared into the blossom on the cherry tree. M nursed the bird in her lap. The tiny eyes, when they opened, were alert. She turned her head from side to side but seemed content to stay where she was. After fifteen minutes, when her breathing had settled down, we put her on a branch of the cherry tree, praying that she hadn't broken a wing. After a few minutes she flew off into another tree. We didn't see the hubby again but he must have been somewhere near. No question of handing back wedding rings with that pair.

Merula's niece Claire, who lives in France, brought her four-year-old French son, Samuel, to see us today. A bright, beautiful, good-natured boy with a charming smile and very white, tiny, French teeth. Well, of course they are French teeth but there is something distinctly continental about them. I remember that in a drawer somewhere I had three toy magnets which I eventually found and gave him. This was a big success, as was the fountain throwing up the greenish pond water.

It has been an enjoyable simple day. We drove to the Durleighmarsh Farm shop and came back loaded with good bread (disastrously irresistible when new), beef tomatoes that actually taste like tomatoes, spring onions, pickles and marvellous coffee ice-cream. Having the shop to ourselves we could call out to each other—'Raspberry vinegar? Celery? What about some cider?' 'Not if it is going to go to your knees!'—as if we owned the place. And then to step outside into sunlight, country views and air without a whiff of petrol. '... It was, you may say, satisfactory.'

Tuesday 16 April
On waking this morning I thought how lovely it would be to have a tame bird again. There has been Percy, a South African grey parrot who lived with us for about twenty-five years, gave us a lot of laughs and painful nips, could recite the first two lines of a Hamlet soliloquy—'O what a rogue and peasant slave am I! Is it not monstrous that this player here'—except that he substituted 'parrot' for 'player', followed by gales of laughter; he also ripped sitting-room curtains to shreds. He finally died, nearly featherless, of cirrhosis of the liver, in the arms of Stanley Hall the wig-maker. There was also a small aviary of tropical birds—ranging from various Australian finches to Mexican hummingbirds—which I started on returning from Sri Lanka; but I used to get so depressed at the little tragedies I regularly found on my return home after a week or two away that I gave it all up. Obviously the bird thought stemmed from the bullfinch incident on Sunday coupled with a passage I read yesterday in Admiral Lord Cochrane's autobiography, written in 1859.

Cochrane, as a midshipman, served during the Napoleonic wars in a frigate in Norwegian waters. They had on board a parrot which nearly drove the first lieutenant mad, as it imitated exactly the bosun's whistle and was endlessly piping out contradictory orders, which were immediately obeyed by the men. On one occasion, in return for hospitality ashore, the officers invited a party of Norwegian townspeople aboard. A 'chair' was rigged to hoist them up the ship's side. A lady was in mid-air when the parrot piped 'Let her go!', which the sailors did, and the poor woman had to be saved from drowning.

No, I mustn't have another bird in spite of always feeling an empathy with them. There was a baby owl in Sri Lanka which had fallen from its nest which I fed with bits of chewed-up raw meat on the end of a matchstick. Life was a touch-and-go affair for several days, but one evening when I visited him (her?), he (she?) gave a just audible hoot and I knew all was well. The owl was about four inches high when I last saw him and I left him in the care of the nice intelligent boy who had brought him to me in the first place. The owl lived with the boy and his parents in a jungle village for about eighteen months before spreading wings and leaving. A message was sent me by someone in Colombo who knew about it.

One April we rented a very simple cottage in Galaxidhion, on the sea just below Delphi. Almost immediately after our arrival we were befriended by a dusty, reddish-brown, clucking old hen. Each morning we would see her, about a hundred yards away, scurrying

216

along the broken-down road to join us for breakfast. She sat herself beside me on a stone bench in the scrap of garden. She never demanded anything, just affection. Two days before we left she spotted my return from the village and ran towards me. She suddenly stopped with fright, gave a squawk and fled in the opposite direction. I was carrying a stick, which she had never seen me do before. Someone must have been maltreating her. Never saw her again to say goodbye. Parting with animals is awful: no explanations possible.

It has been a dull day only enlivened by a letter asking if I am a patron of a theatre group which is now teaching its pupils how to see 'the inner light'. With the letter was a broadsheet on which my name was printed (incorrectly spelt of course) as a patron. I had forgotten all about the venture which, if I remember correctly, was set up four or five years ago in an attempt to help post-drama-school students. It seems to have changed principal and intentions more than once. Eventually I tracked down, on the telephone, the person in charge—a nice-sounding young woman who was fairly shimmering with inner light—and asked her to remove my name as a patron. She sounded relieved and said my name had been removed a year ago anyway.

Collapse of stout party.

Wednesday 17 April

A warm day. Arrived in town 11.45. To bank to order lire for Lake Como jaunt in May. Lunched at Garrick, sitting next to Derek Bond. Acutely embarrassed that his name escaped me until, happily, he mentioned Cavalcanti's film of *Nicholas Nickleby* in which he had starred.

The object of my London visit, apart from bank and dining tonight with Sam Beazley, was to go to the National Portrait Gallery. Quentin Stevenson, always original and interesting in his approach to the arts, had sent me a card a week ago recommending a visit to the gallery but *only* to look at busts and statuary. He had done this recently and found it very rewarding. So I set off from the Garrick to follow in his footsteps—but no such luck. The police had cordoned off the bottom of St Martin's Lane, Charing Cross Road and part of Trafalgar Square. A suspected terrorist bomb. People stood in groups by the police tapes, gazing and waiting—but for what? An explosion? Or at any rate for some sort of drama. Tourists, with their open maps, were obviously very confused and kept revolving in a nonplussed way. Buses were nose to tail, empty and idling.

At 10 p.m., while Sam and I were toying with our crème brûlées, a bomb went off in The Boltons near Earl's Court. No casualties. The work, they say, of the IRA.

218

Friday 19 April
Kevin Brownlow and I lunched at the Connaught yesterday and he gave me a copy of his biography of David Lean which is published today. It is a vast tome, over 750 pages. I read it in typescript a couple of years ago and I was impressed. It is undoubtedly a definitive work. The book is in sharp focus, sympathetic, readable and few punches are pulled; other people's punches, perhaps I should say. Kevin shares, of course, David's passion and knowledge of film. Two newspapers have asked me to review it but I couldn't face attempting that. Apart from having other things I must get on with, I don't want to go through all the Lean sagas again; once in a lifetime has been enough.

The only excitement today has been rescuing a drowsy bumble-bee crawling slowly across the floor. Japheth pointed at it but kept his distance. The bumble-bees are with us again now the big cherry outside the kitchen has sprung into dazzling flower. The whiter than white daffodils opposite my study are the best they have ever been. It all feels rather A. E. Housman-like, but Hampshire not Shropshire.

Sunday 21 April
Only got round to opening yesterday's mail this morning. In it was an invitation for me

(name incorrectly spelt, as usual) and my 'partner' from 'The Selina Scott Show' to join the *QE* 2 in May, sailing to New York from Southampton. First-class accommodation offered 'and food'. Glad about the food. No mention of how one gets back. All I would have to do would be to submit to some TV interviews and help celebrate 100 years of cinema. Of course I shall write back politely declining but I am tempted to reply that my 'partner' for the past fifty-eight years has been my wife and asking if that would be OK. Also our combined ages come to 163, which might be embarrassing. The real pleasure of a transatlantic crossing on a big liner is tramping round and round the promenade deck kidding yourself you are being healthy. M would be unable to do that now—she gets seasick, anyway, if she sees a ripple—and I wouldn't enjoy being closeted in seminars on significant film. We appreciate the offer but shall drop our anchor in Lake Como (d.v.) in May. Vincent and Coral Price would have leapt at the opportunity and enjoyed every minute; I think their greatest pleasure in life was to be at sea on a luxurious freebie.

Warm-hearted neighbours, Mr and Mrs Crace, came for a pre-lunch drink. Alas, they are moving from their pretty house down the lane to be in the bright lights and all the action of Petersfield.

It has been a beautiful sunny day, almost warm enough to sit out, but I have developed a nasty spluttering cough and spent most of the afternoon in bed. No question of going to Mass and passing on my germs to the parish.

Monday 22 April

Preparations for summer fêtes are well in hand, judging from the number of raffle tickets that are sent me. Six booklets this morning, all from charities I've never heard of; worthy causes, no doubt, but I find it all an irritating form of blackmail and time-consuming.

Rain drips and so does my nose; I feel rather better than I did yesterday but think I may return to bed in the afternoon. M has gone to the local nursery garden to stock up with plants to stick in pots all over the place. It's a good sign—her being active outside the house. Dido and Michaelmas the cat have coiled themselves up side by side on the sofa and look like small plump cushions. Japheth has spread himself out lengthways and is casting melancholic eyes on a damp grey world.

It is nearly eleven and I have neither shaved nor dressed, just shuffled around in my old, frayed, blue towelling dressing-gown. It's comfortable and warm enough. Perhaps it is the right day to read a Shakespeare play with which I'm not familiar. *The Two Noble Kinsmen* perhaps. I have only read that once, I think. I remember liking much of it and being struck by its visual possibilities in staging. There is a suggestion of Inigo Jones about it.

Looking at *Two Noble Kinsmen* (I, i) I find:

'Now you may take him,
Drunk with his victory.'
'And his army *full of bread* and sloth.'

That's not very far removed from *Hamlet*, III, iii:

He took my father grossly, *full of bread*,

and, a few lines later:

When he is *drunk* asleep or in his rage.

Perhaps I am getting light-headed with my heavy cold. A cup of steaming hot Bovril and bed for a few hours.

Tuesday 23 April
A request this morning from a ladies' football team for a signed football shirt.

Shakespeare's birthday/death day. Also Turner's birthday. There has been the usual run-up to WS's birthday of hate letters and facetious articles suggesting he never existed. Tell that to the shades of Ben Jonson, Kit Marlowe and all.

Feeling a bit better than yesterday but still have a violent head cold. Back in bed in the afternoon, accompanied by *The Two Noble Kinsmen*. I'm afraid I'm not up to the knotty language. ('Please try later', as the BT lady says.) I'm desperately in need of a laugh. Kicked the *2 Nob.K'men* out of bed and welcomed *David Copperfield*, which I can't have read for fifty years. Found it immediately rewarding. Besides, it has all those pretty and funny pictures to look at, which is just what you want when snuggled, child-like, in bed.

Down for a stiff Horse's Neck at 18.30. During dinner we played CD of Beethoven's Piano Sonata No. 32—for me the greatest piece of music I know. Life, death, all turmoils, sorrows and happinesses seem to be resolved whenever I hear it. Japheth sat himself quietly at my side on the banquette. Shortly before the end he lowered his great white head gently on my shoulder.

I'm glad I'm not having to undergo any surgery just now. Today's press is full of photographs of the Princess of Wales, in operating-theatre gear and pale make-up, sitting in on a serious operation. We are told she is doing the rounds of several hospitals. 'Pardon me, Your Royal Highness, but this is *my* hernia and I don't want anyone to stitch it up except the surgeon. Another whiff of gas, nurse, if you don't mind. And leave out the Calèche Parfum.'

Thursday 25 April

Thoughts for the Day? Nonsense; there are no thoughts for the day. Panic is setting in about the speech I have to make in Eastbourne on Sunday night. If only I could come up with a gripping opening line I would feel easier. All that has floated my way so far is— 'Shakespeare, in Henry V, has a brief phrase, "Old men forget". ' It is horribly true, as every old person knows, but what would be even more disturbing would be 'Old men remember!', for once they start remembering how the hell do you put a stop to them? And by 'them' I mean me.

A gentle chill wind is taking away the cherry blossom after its gaudy flaunting and many of the daffodils are beginning to look like crumpled up tax demands. M has been to Hillier's Nurseries again and come back with a great variety of parsley seeds, for which we have no space. Rabbits will be delighted and feel encouraged. I've never heard of a parsley called Turnip Rooted Omega, which I see among the shopping. It seems you grate the root for sprinkling over all sorts of autumnal dishes. There is enough grating going on in this house as it is, what with nutmeg, lemon zest and brick-hard chunks of Parmesan.

Keith Baxter comes to dinner tonight. Next week he is off to Washington for a couple of months to play the Duke in *Measure for Measure,* a fine but tricky part. Roger Livesey was admirable in it (in Guthrie's 1930s production) with Charles Laughton as Angelo, Flora Robson as Isabella and James Mason as Claudio. It was one of the best Shakespeare productions I have ever seen and it played to almost empty houses. The thirties looked on *Measure for Measure* as an obscure, unfamiliar play. The danger nowadays is that it too often provides a field day for Freudians. Keith, I'm sure will tackle it straight and for what it is worth—which is great drama.

Today 30 lb of explosive was found under Hammersmith Bridge. Presumably it was intended to do as much damage to life and property as possible. It's odd it wasn't detonated for the Boat Race.

Telephoned Valerie Profumo to ask how she and Jack had fared on their Moroccan holiday (from which they have just returned), to discuss what clothes we should take to Lake Como—ridiculous to ask Valerie that, as she replies 'Oh, a tatty old pair of darned slacks,' when you know she is going to turn up looking a million dollars—and what Jack thinks we should be prepared for by way of household tipping. It would be horrible to underdo it, but we also wish to avoid ostentatious over-tipping. They are going to make discreet inquiries. We also chatted about 'elevenses'; I said that, sadly, I have had to give up coffee and now usually have a Bovril. Valerie is a lady who knows a thing or two and she said she and

Jack are enthusiastic hot Bovril drinkers with a slug of port in it.

Roll on eleven tomorrow morning.

Saturday 27 April
Valerie is entirely to blame—port in Bovril at 11 a.m. yesterday flattened me out for the afternoon, but the weather was so gorgeous I was able to loll in the sun out of doors. In fact it got too hot and eventually I was glad of the relief of getting back in the house.

Norman Lewis's *The World, The World* arrived from Heywood Hill this morning. I shall start on it tonight and leave *Copperfield*, which I am loving, until we go on holiday. Lewis's *Naples 44* was one of the most engaging books to come out of the 39/45 hostilities, with a spot-on evocation of southern Italy which vividly revived wartime memories. When choosing holiday books I need to be 100 per cent sure I'm taking something I'm not going to regret. Last summer Ruskin's *The Crown of Wild Olive* was a weary mistake.

A cease-fire has been brokered between Israel and Hezbollah. Thank God. It came into effect in the early hours of this morning.

In spite of a fairly strong westerly wind it was warm enough to eat lunch out of doors, not on the patio but sitting, a little hard on our backsides, at a picnic table, facing a paddock with sheep (guests) and brightly sprouting dandelions (indigenous). Listened to 'Any Questions', lowering our heads closer and closer to the radio as the batteries slowly failed. Lady politicians faded to whispering sweet nothings.

Sunday 28 April
One of the depressing things about arriving in a fifth-rate hotel is the knowledge that you are going to find bent wire coat-hangers jangling in a rickety wardrobe. The hangers will barely have the strength to support a shirt, let alone a suit. A far cry from that to the way-up-market De Vere Grand Hotel at Eastbourne where decently shaped wooden coat-hangers are plentifully supplied, but they are of the kind which have a solid nail through the top instead of a hook. You go fishing in the air for minutes, holding up the weight of your clothes, while trying to make a satisfactory connection with the little metal contraption which should take the head of the nail. I suppose, from the hotel's point of view, this discourages guests from petty thieving. I would rather do without all the posh little knick-knacks on offer in the glossy bathrooms and see the money saved go on old-fashioned coat-hangers.

I have been provided (courtesy of Penguin Books) with an extremely nice suite, high up, with a fine view of the sea; but it was hermetically sealed until the housekeeper crawled along the floor to release various secret

227

catches. Then the sea air fairly blew in, fresh and sunny. Before going down to dinner Christopher and Debbie Sinclair-Stevenson, Tony Lacey and a few other Penguins came for drinks (again courtesy Penguins) in my sitting-room. My eye fell on a couple of bowls of what I took to be cocktail nibbles and I proffered these around. They turned out to be bowls of pot-pourri.

Then downstairs to make a disastrous speech to a hundred booksellers. I lost heart within a few minutes, decided my audience wasn't remotely interested (why should they be?) or amused (small hope) and I gradually petered out. Must avoid these occasions. Was always bad at it and now getting worse. How the hell would I manage as an actor nowadays?

Horrible news came through from Tasmania of the deliberate shooting down of thirty-four people by a deranged young man. Oh, the world, the world.

Monday 29 April
Woke at seven to a halcyon day (if halcyon days can occur outside winter), to the squeals of a few seagulls wheeling around and the distant sound of a car. Even the car noise was acceptable. When breakfast came I was glad I had ordered *two* boiled eggs—I had dallied with the thought of one—as they were the smallest chicken eggs I have ever seen. David Pike collected me at 10.30 and the drive past

228

Beachy Head, the Downs and Cuckmere Haven was as satisfying as ever. Near Chichester dark clouds gathered and it turned cold.

Sorry to read in the papers that Derek Jacobi, who was to open at the Chichester Festival Theatre tonight—in *Love for Love*—has been whisked into hospital for the removal of an appendix. Wretched for him and a nightmare, I imagine, for his understudy.

In the evening we were fairly glued to the box by the account of the restoration of Holbein's 'The Ambassadors' at the National Gallery. It crossed my mind once or twice that I might appreciate Mr John Prescott's views on painting, with his gravelly voice, rather than those—but not all—of the cognoscenti.

Tuesday 30 April
M, in one of her ruthless moods, has decided she wants an ailing juniper tree felled and various other shrubs garrotted. So our Mrs Spurdle and Mr Turrell are sawing, dragging and piling branches on the wheelbarrow (many journeys), preparing for a monstrous bonfire which will scare or choke our neighbours.

MAY 1996

Wednesday 1 May

A bomb scare at noon, just as I arrived at my bank. Piccadilly roped off from Fortnum's for about three hundred yards westwards. Drew money and fortified myself with a Bloody Mary and gulls' eggs at Wiltons.

After that to National Portrait Gallery to carry out Quentin's idea (in which I was frustrated a week ago by another bomb scare) of avoiding the paintings and disciplining oneself to just look at the sculpture. After twenty minutes I found myself attracted irresistibly to the portraits—particularly in the arts section.

Of the busts I looked at I was struck by the Glynn Williams stone carving of Lord Annan and Epstein's bronze of Lucian Freud, which is very fawn-like. The most striking portrait, for my money, is Michael Taylor's oil of Julian Bream. For ten minutes I sat and gazed at it and felt I knew Bream. What surprised me was the rather formidable, almost morose, look in the eye. Peggy Ashcroft was devoted to him (as a guitarist, friend and fellow cricketer) and many others speak of him with great affection, but there is in that portrait something different, something a little uncomfortable. That is always reassuring in an artist's face.

The portrait of Max Wall by Maggi Hambling and Julian Trevelyan's self-portrait gave me pleasure. The latter is sort of frivolous, colourful, mocking and rather touching. I was caught out for a moment by stumbling against Liz Frink's head of me which I hadn't seen for some years. It looked somehow smaller than I had remembered it and not quite so imperious but it is still grossly bull-necked. It would need a size 26 shirt collar I think. An elderly man—well, nearly my age—did a slow double take when he saw me look at it, so I suppose there must be a likeness. Fearing he was going to comment I moved on. He followed, with curiosity, but never spoke; he sidled up to anything I stopped to look at and seeped off a little gas. I quickened my pace, which was necessary.

To Walton Street where I bought M two elegant, plain, linen nightgowns at the little Scandinavian shop Nor Style. The saleslady, good at her job, tried to sell me everything in the shop. Then to Issey Miyake and treated myself to a flashy but smart necktie; bright and dark blue smudged stripes. Now that I have it I doubt if I shall dare wear it.

Tonight Piers Paul Read and Emily dine with me at the Berkeley.

*   *   *

That was enjoyable except for the fact that I

have developed toothache. The Berkeley dining-room proved blissfully quiet, service was first class and food—what I could chew—good.

Friday 3 May
Merula joined me in London yesterday morning. After lunch we went to see Mr Van Oldenborgh about our eyes; he advised M to wait another year before doing anything about her cataract and we decided to postpone deciding about an operation to my blind eye until after I get back from Italy in June.

From Wimpole Street we went to the O'Shea gallery in Mount Street to see the exhibition of Peter Coke's remarkable shell work. The flower arrangements are superb. His patience and skill are staggering. For a couple of weeks each year, usually in August, he sets off for northern France taking our friend and neighbour Henryetta with him and together they comb the beaches for shells. I can see them, at every low tide, bent double, with behinds in the air, peering, delicately picking, rinsing, and triumphantly returning to their hotel with dripping bags of highly coloured shells to be washed yet again in hand-basins.

We spent Thursday evening with Alan Bennett, who has just returned from The Hague, where he had gone to see the Vermeers. He was thrilled to bits with them and as he had gone with fellow trustees of the National

233

Gallery he had easy viewing.

This morning we did some household shopping for the Bank Holiday weekend (they come thick and fast at this time of year) and left town at eleven. Bitterly cold north wind. I had forgotten to feed the fish when I set off on Wednesday; when I got to the pond this afternoon my dear, docile koi were behaving like angry piranha.

The Tories have lost getting on for six hundred seats in the local council elections, as predicted. I can't whip up much interest in any of that. All I pray is that no government, now or in the future, will be so mad as to destroy our movement towards Europe.

Henryetta, a staunch vegan, comes down this evening from her hideaway on the Hangers to sample M's Risotto Primavera, which I know will be excellent. I can smell it already and I think it deserves a rather nice hock.

Monday 6 May
A beautiful morning but the air quite sharp in the nostrils, stiffening the bristles. Walked barefoot round the pond before getting dressed; all was quiet and idyllic, the Bank Holiday traffic presumably having reached its destination on Saturday. The contra-flow will start tonight. The viburnum is out in rich white globes, scenting the air.

Last night we watched 'A History of English Art', presented by Andrew Graham-Dixon.

This episode covered Hogarth, Reynolds, Gainsborough and Stubbs. All very admirable but I am beginning to wish the words Jane and Austen had never been heard of. I got the point Mr Graham-Dixon was making but I fear it could be easily misleading to refer to Miss Austen while showing portraits of fashionable, aristocratic, high-bewigged ladies of the mid eighteenth century. Since all those Prejudices, Sensibilities and Emmas have been offered for our constant entertainment poor Jane Austen's name is evoked on every social occasion. Before long we shall have Mansfield Park and Northanger football clubs.

The most moving painting shown last night was, for my taste, Stubbs's 'Zebra in an English Glade'. The animal, brilliant in his black and white stripes, standing in beautiful profile, looked stiffly perplexed and lost among all the dappled greenery. A stranger in a strange land. At least he wasn't in a zoo.

Other programmes seemed to be offering the usual weekend dollops of scatological humour. After flicking remote-control buttons for a few minutes I returned with relief and pleasure to Norman Lewis's *The World, The World*.

*   *   *

Sat in the sun for half an hour, drinking in the light greenness of everything, ruminating and wandering idly in my thoughts.

The Lavender Hill Mob is being shown on TV this evening but I won't be watching it. (If only I had received £1 each time one of the Ealing comedies was shown I would be a rich man. My contract didn't cover mechanical reproduction.) It was a good film, I think; well over forty years old now and mercifully it only lasted an hour and a half. Stanley Holloway and I got on exceedingly well and became good friends. He was always genial, easy-going and meticulously professional.

Ealing Studios never succeeded in killing me in spite of some quite good tries, the first of which was during the making of Lavender Hill. Rehearsing a brief scene in which Stanley and I were required to escape from the top of the Eiffel Tower, the director (Charlie Crichton) said, 'Alec, there is a trap door over there— where it says Workmen Only—I'd like you to run to it, open it and start running down the spiral staircase. Stanley will follow.' So I did as asked. A very dizzying sight to the ground greeted me. But I completed half a spiral before I noticed that three feet in front of me the steps suddenly ceased—broken off. I sat down promptly where I was and cautiously started to shift myself back to the top, warning Stanley to get out of the way.

'What the hell are you doing?' the director yelled. 'Down! Further down!'

'Further down is eternity,' I called back.

Stanley and I regained the panoramic view of Paris pale and shaking. No one had checked up on the staircase and no one apologized; that wasn't Ealing policy.

Tuesday 7 May
Other people's dreams, recounted over the breakfast table, are inclined to be either embarrassing or boring, and are always too formless to be understood. Dreams are private affairs and yet I woke this morning knowing I wanted to record a dream I had last night.

The venue was Brighton, on the upper level of the Marine Parade. The time was fairly early in the morning but it could have been now or in the thirties. The weather was perfection; in fact it was a 'halcyon day' such as I recorded in Eastbourne a week ago. Coming towards me, walking vigorously, was a very attractive tall young woman dressed stylishly in pale blue, the colour of the sky. There was no one else about and there wasn't a breath of wind. The girl was smiling to herself but battling with a violent wind which touched only her. The silk scarf she wore flapped and snapped like a flag in a gale and she had to use a hand to cling on to her cloche hat. She didn't look at me as she passed and I felt no pressure of the wind that engulfed her. I turned to look at her; strangely she was already a hundred yards away and she looked somehow different—older perhaps, more stately and in darker clothes. *C'est tout.* I can make nothing of it, yet I know I enjoyed the experience.

Late in the morning I turned over yet again the film script of *The Cherry Orchard* by Michael Cacoyannis. It is more filmic, I think, than the one Lindsay Anderson hoped to do in Russia three or four years ago. Also the character of Firs, the butler, emerges more satisfactorily. Idly it came into my head that the point about knighthoods for British actors is to enable them to go to Hollywood to play butlers in glossy movies. And now I am not sure if that *aperçu* is mine—as I believe, or picked up from someone else. Awful not to know for sure if you are plagiarizing or being wildly original. I shall give myself the benefit of the doubt.

Firs again. I remembered a little school exercise book in which I made occasional jottings and I was sure there would be something about *The Cherry Orchard* in it. I was right. Under the date of 17 January 1994 I find: 'Last night I woke at 02.30 thinking about Firs in the party scene. I said to myself, "I must tell Lindsay that I think it important that the old boy should sit down for a bit during the dancing: (a) he is not feeling very well and (b) he disapproves of the guests, whom he considers vulgar upstarts."' So in the morning I telephoned Mander and Mitchenson, who have a great photographic collection and know everything knowable about the theatre. I asked if they had any photograph of Firs in the 1958 Moscow Arts production, which I had seen, or, more importantly, of the 1904 Stanislavski production, which was the first. They got back to me within the hour; yes, they had one of the party scene in 1904. 'You can pick out Firs,' they said, 'but he is not awfully clear. He appears to be sitting.' Odd. They sent me the photograph, and I am afraid that after a day or two I decided it wasn't Firs who was sitting. In another photograph of Firs in the same production he is quite clearly, and surprisingly, wearing Mongolian boots with turned-up toes. Chekhov loathed his performance.

After the nine o'clock news we watched a short documentary about John Davis of the Rank Organization, 'The Man who Destroyed the British Film Industry'. Disappointing. I had hoped it would be harder hitting. Davis was an objectionable man. I only met him once but it was enough to get his flavour. He came on to the set at Pinewood where I was making a very indifferent film for Rank. 'Give us some laughs, Alec. Give us some pratfalls.' After the film was finished he inserted a shot of someone else's legs, in my trousers, doing just that. When I saw the film the audience groaned with contempt at that moment, as did I. Comedy and accountancy don't go hand in hand.

Thursday 9 May
A man with a shock of strikingly white hair,

which was being tugged in the wind, stood outside his scarlet car and looked at the house. For a moment I thought he was Marius Goring and I went to invite him in. But, no, he was from the waterworks and only here to tell us we were about to be cut off for a few hours. He delivered his news with an apologetic smile.

Irene W telephoned, bubbling with enthusiasm, having just returned from her first visit to the Lake District. Ten minutes later Sam Beazley got on the buzzer, equally joyous, having got back yesterday from a jaunt (sketching and painting) somewhere in the High Sierras. Here, all that is on offer today is a blue sky with rather rough-looking clouds driven by an icy northern wind.

Small birds—tits, finches and a robin—which I was watching out of my study window, all happily busy foraging, suddenly disappeared as if they had been un-created. Couldn't think why. Then a greater spotted woodpecker settled on the nut dispenser and gorged himself for five minutes. After he had gone it took quite a while for the other birds to return. He had destroyed their serenity, I suppose, but he was a glorious sight to human eyes.

Saturday 11 May
A glossy young crow tried to get into the house yesterday, perhaps a dozen or more times. He either bashed himself at the windows or

fluttered against them or, perched on a balcony railing, peered in while squawking. Maybe he caught his reflection in the glass and thought it was a mate. This morning, far too early, he was at it again, but 'as the day goes on' (BBC weather forecast) he seems to be tiring. He's going to be a bloody nuisance if he keeps it up.

House martins are twirling around, prospecting, but they never build here, although they often make settlements less than a mile away. Someone said that our sandy soil doesn't suit them.

This afternoon we watched the Manchester United and Liverpool confrontation at Wembley. It all seemed rather even paced, good tempered, and Cantona scored the only goal—for Man. Utd. I am no aficionado of the game but it seemed to me there was a touch of genius in the sheer direction and power of Cantona's goal—which was made from quite a distance. I hope the hooligan who abused him last year was squirming somewhere on a bar stool. And now it appears that a Liverpudlian fan spat at Cantona when he received the trophy.

Monday 13 May
M has just come back from the doctor. She is suffering from giddy spells. She has been on Stemetils—one a day—for about three weeks—but the dosage is to be increased. Mark and Marigold Kingston were coming for

next weekend but I have put them off, as even if M is feeling better by then I'm sure it would be unwise for her to be busying about the house. Fingers crossed that all will have cleared up totally by this time next week; I couldn't bear to do a last-minute call-off to Drue's Como invitation for the second year running. The doctor says it would be probably OK for her to fly but he strongly advises against small boats. Boat trips, I know, are planned.

The crow came banging at the window again. I drove him away with wild gestures and now I feel horribly mean. In the past hour I have learned he is probably half tame. A local garage had befriended a crow and he disappeared a few days ago. What to do? He would be impossible to catch to redeliver to his old stomping ground.

Wednesday 15 May
In spite of bright sunlight and nearly all the trees suddenly in leaf, yesterday was depressing. Just as I was about to leave for London M had a nasty spell of vertigo. Mrs Spurdle was here and proposed staying the night so I was persuaded to go. As soon as I reached town I altered various business plans to enable me to come back this afternoon. Yesterday it looked very much as if Italy would have to be cancelled. As often, when feeling anxious and low-spirited, I got in touch with Alan B and asked him to spend the evening

with me. He is always sympathetic and reassuring and never thinks it comforting to pour out his own troubles, which many people do.

We went to the Berkeley (I rather wanted an Indian or Thai meal but Alan shies off the East) and as I was early I sat in an armchair in the lobby from which I had a good view of the main entrance. This proved rewarding. People staying in the hotel swung through the door without a thought for others, wearing a proud air of ownership. Some very well-dressed ladies flounced out, wearing below their silken skirts huge white sneakers. Their self-confidence was enviable. Visitors unfamiliar with their surroundings plopped into the hall like goldfish thrown into a glass bowl, their mouths slightly open, their eyes popping, not at all sure which way to swim. Alan's arrival—he was wearing a sports jacket, blue shirt with a crumply collar and twisted string of a tie— didn't cause a twitch of an eyebrow. I rejoice that he brings Yorkshire and Camden Town with him wherever he goes.

This morning, Wednesday, I telephoned M at 08.30 and she sounded brighter, having had a good night and no recurrence of nausea. To Roux Brothers for household shopping and to the bank to collect a wodge of lire. Italian banknotes have got smaller in recent years but I miss the huge, thick, high-denomination notes which looked like blankets. There was something soft about them, almost woolly, and you felt you really were getting your money's worth; the money's worth was probably only about £10.

Bought Anthony Powell's recent *Journals, 1987–89*, which I hope will keep me amused until it is time to get back to *Copperfield*.

David Pike drove me down in the early afternoon. Since yesterday he has invested in a new Peugeot; white, roomier and smoother than his old red rattle-bones. He is a marvellously good driver; I don't know a better. Somehow he manages to be acutely aware of everything that is happening on the road, in front and to the rear.

Merula looks much like her old self again but is being sensibly cautious about how she moves. If she continues to improve over the next few days I think we'll manage to get away on the 24th.

Thursday 16 May
A cold northerly wind, clouds low, and a lot lower still an army 'copter keeps skimming over the house in an inquisitive way. Cherry blossom is scattered everywhere like dirty confetti. There is a smell of much-needed rain in the air.

I forgot to record a pleasant half hour yesterday morning at the William Nicholson exhibition in Cork Street. Everything was covetable but I was mesmerized by a painting of a gold jug and another of a pewter jug. The metals appeared to be metal in a very convincing way and yet the colours used were greens, yellows, browns, greys, black and white; above all white. Superb work.

The foreman of the waterworks was expected here half an hour ago; I sit at my desk a little impatiently, tapping my feet. He wants to show me where they intend to dig to lay a new supply pipe to a horse trough in the paddock. The trough has been there for over forty years, working quite satisfactorily. They spent several hours last week probing for the pipe; they might just as well have used a dowser. It's going to cost someone—probably me—quite a sum of money. It seems I'm responsible for the upkeep of the pipes for two hundred yards.

*   *   *

Well, the man came. He was perfectly agreeable, showed me his plan—which turned out to be less complicated than I had feared—and said they will start work next week. How much it is going to cost he didn't mention; fearful, perhaps, that I might have a heart attack. Water pressure is going to be greatly increased, which I can't think necessary.

Stacking away some old newspapers for recycling, my eye fell on something which

245

I instantly recognized—my own name. It occurred in a review of an American book about the paranormal. It simply said, 'Alec Guinness possesses second sight.' News to me.

At last, rain. Not heavy but decently steady; puddles are forming in the usual places in the drive. Two or three pigeons are sloshing around and I think I hear a thrush.

Friday 17 May
Dido saw off a pretty fox cub but didn't pursue. She is now curled up in front of the fire, looking like an ammonite.

A card this morning from a friend who lives in Scotland and always has a good tale to pass on. He once told me of the Catholic Bishop of Argyll and the Western Isles who said, 'We once had a Conservative candidate for the Isle of Barra. He told the islanders that if returned as their representative he would bring work to the islands. Naturally he lost his deposit.'

My own day has been workless and idle, except for the second most boring thing in the world, which is arranging for a MoT test, renewal of car licence, insurance, etc. The first most boring thing is signing photographs; I disciplined myself to do that for half an hour, having neglected a nasty-looking pile of envelopes for weeks. Oh, to be abroad or at any rate elsewhere on this cold, grey, sullen day. It isn't even raining.

I rather would entreat thy company
To see the wonders of the world abroad
Than, living dully sluggardiz'd at home,
Wear out thy youth with shapeless
    idleness.

Two Gents. of Verona, I, i

M has been steady now for two days, with no sense of nausea, so there is a good chance that this time next week we shall be touching down at Milan's Lenate airport, where surely it must be warmer.

Saturday 18 May
An unexpected gift of John Updike's *The Same Door*, his first volume of short stories (1959), arrived this morning. Apart from the pleasure of possessing them they will make admirable air-travel reading and the book is slim enough to go comfortably into a briefcase. The Dickens is rather chunky and will have to be packed. For once I hope to manage a short holiday without taking everything I own.

Reading Anthony Powell's *Journals* with interest. His account of his audience with the Queen when he received his CH (in 1988) coincides exactly—with the exception of a name or two and Hampshire supplanting Somerset—with my own, ditto, in 1994. I wonder if Her Majesty gets tired of playing that particular scene; after all, it has been a long run. On the other hand it may not be too bad, as there are only a few handfuls of CHs, which is what makes it such a desirable honour. As yet I haven't had an opportunity to wear mine; just as well, as I doubt if I could get comfortably into my white tie and tails. Perhaps its first public showing will be on the lid of my coffin. That goes for my Hon. DLitt. (Oxon) gown as well, a beautiful red wool with dove-grey silk facings. Had to buy it, of course—£90 I think. Cambridge University only *lent* their gowns and caps, and they were very particular about getting them back. 'Please make sure you return your dress before leaving the premises' sort of thing.

In the evening we watched an excellent documentary about Alexander the Great, put together by Tony Spawforth, archaeologist and a likeable personality. It was largely a search for Alexander's burial place and, oddly enough, not unentertaining. I particularly liked the medieval painting of Alexander being lowered into the sea in a glass globe to study the denizens of the deep. The spurts of dramatic music were intrusive, distracting and, as always, tiresome. If people wanted music they only had to flick to BBC1 where there were three uninterrupted hours of, God save us, Eurovision Song Contest. Alexander's dust could have slept in quiet peace. Hamlet says:

Alexander died, Alexander was buried. Alexander returneth to dust, the dust is earth, of earth we make loam, and why of that loam whereto he was converted might they not stop a beer-barrel?

Monday 20 May
An orange-coloured snake, four feet long, has escaped from Bedales School. Or so we are told. It is said to be an Australian beast, not venomous but very aggressive. From our living-room we can see the edge of Bedales playing-fields, about a mile away. As I have a dislike of all ophidia I am keeping a sharp lookout; but it is doubtful if any furless creature could survive this bitter wind.

'The pancakes were naught but the mustard was good.' That nagged me all morning and I couldn't place it until my eye fell on C. T. Onions's *Shakespeare Glossary—As You Like It*—which led me to rummage for some random jottings on Shakespeare made a year ago. Not sure what I had in mind; perhaps something about how rewarding some of the smallest parts can be. Not quite applicable but it amused me again to come across Marlowe's line from *Tamburlaine*, 'Holla, ye pampered jades of Asia!' followed by Shakespeare's glorious send-up—'Hollow pamper'd jades of Asia!' I can see Shakespeare's company falling about with suppressed giggles in rehearsal. Maybe Shakespeare didn't write 'hollow' but the actor playing Pistol couldn't resist it. Such things happen.

M has put on my desk a little stone vase of lilies of the valley which she has gleaned from round and about.

Tuesday 21 May
To P'field in the morning for M to visit chiropodist and me to go to the excellent One Tree bookshop. I got paperbacks of *Tom Jones* and *Great Expectations*, both of which M wants to reread. To opticians and bought some pricey sunglasses which I hope will be needed at the end of the week.

A happy letter from Keith Baxter in Washington DC where he is rehearsing *Measure for Measure* in temperatures in the eighties. A call from my agent saying *The Cherry Orchard* film is still on the cards and that they have already photographed shots of cherry blossom somewhere.

Eileen (Atkins) started rehearsals yesterday for *The Master Builder* at the National with Big Van—the current theatrical endearment for the great Vanessa Redgrave. She sounds very on top of things, which is marvellous, considering she has been pretty unwell for some months. A very resilient woman. A week or two back Micky Gough sent me a p.c. of a Victorian painting of an aged camel driver and a very white-skinned lady, with huge eyes, who was swathed coyly in diaphanous chiffon; they and their camel were having a little rest at an oasis. On the back of the card he has written,

'Good parts for you and Eileen?'

I have only seen *The Master Builder* once, when Ralph, Peggy and Wendy Hiller did it at the National. Larry Olivier and I went together. Ralph wore some special shoes with electronic gadgetry in the heels so his footsteps made a lot of noise as he walked about upstairs. We were told they cost £700. In the interval the revolve stuck and it took half an hour to sort it out. We remained very apprehensive of its starts and shudders through the rest of the evening. At the end of the performance Larry and I went backstage. When we were leaving his dressing-room Ralph suggested his dresser should show us the way out. Larry declined, saying, 'You forget, old thing, that I was responsible for this theatre. I know every brick in it.' He beckoned me and away we went. Some twenty minutes later we found ourselves in a vast, damp, dripping, ill-lit area under the Thames. Our shouts echoed meaninglessly. A search party picked up the sounds and rescued us. It was a long evening.

Yesterday the pond had small whirlpools of minute tadpoles; today not a sign of them. I hope they have not been gobbled up; tadpoles always amuse and delight, as do frogs.

At six this evening there was a violent hailstorm accompanied by thunder and lightning. The dogs immediately sought human comfort and the protection of cushions on the sofa. The storm only lasted fifteen minutes but three hours later the grass is still pitted with hailstones. And there is a curious sight: dense mist, about ten feet high, is trapped in every fall of the land. A couple of young deer moved slowly into the mist when it rose. It all looks rather ghostly.

Thursday 23 May
A day of packing, unpacking and re-packing. Have thrown out *Pericles* and *Troilus*—there is bound to be some Shakespeare at Casa Ecco if I feel the need of him.

All the millennium talk is getting me down; it's almost as bad as beef talk. I have yet to see any reference to the millennium being a global affair; apart from the Muslims we all more or less use the same dating system. Our insular attitude seems to be confined to ferris wheels, theme parks and a statue or two. The break-up of Christendom proves to have been a greater tragedy than I had realized.

In this house we continue to eat beef when we feel like it, but I see no reason why we should attempt to force-feed the Germans, French and other European nations with our beef when they clearly don't want it and are suspicious of their own. People in this country don't feel obliged to eat French cheese. Our government's talk of reprisals and generally putting a spanner in the works seems to me embarrassingly juvenile. All those TV shots (the same ones night after night) of cattle munching their fodder through iron railings when you know they are going to be slaughtered unnecessarily is hopelessly sad. There must be someone in this land who could think up a sensible, humane and wise solution without bringing us all to the brink of economic war.

There is welcome rain.

Saturday 25 May
At Casa Ecco. It is 11 a.m. and I am sitting at a stone table in a small pergola overlooking sloping lawns and cypress trees to Lake Como, perhaps three hundred feet below. Filtered sunlight and marvellous scents of box, laurel and, maybe, pale mauve irises. The mountains on the far side of the lake are blue-grey and touched with thin cloud. A cock is crowing not far away to the north and is being answered by another to the south; they must be at least half a mile apart. A gentle church bell clunks modestly every half hour and the sound of traffic is decently remote. In fact everything is idyllic and relaxing.

I have lost half the stopping from a back tooth which means my tongue, with a will of its own, is going to tiresomely explore the area until we get back to London and a dentist. I thought it was an unaccountable pip in the breakfast marmalade.

We left home yesterday at 09.30, in rain,

David Pike driving us to the airport. Japheth and Dido looked glum, eyeing the luggage with disapproval, but Michaelmas the cat was totally indifferent, marching around with his tail in the air like an exclamation mark. Met up with Jack and Valerie Profumo at Heathrow. Boarded the plane at 12.15 (scheduled take-off) but sat in it for one and a quarter hours before it took to the air. The BA lunch wasn't bad, the brill mashed up with potato and carrot was enjoyable. We were met at Milan by Drue's admirable chauffeur, Paul. Temperature at Milan 81°. Natasha Spender and Dr John Casey, who are our fellow guests, were on the same plane unbeknown to us.

Tea (of many varieties) on the lawn when we arrived at the villa about 7 p.m. local time. It is an extraordinary and pleasing building, very pink and crenellated—built (on ancient Roman foundations) in the 1860s and much refurbished by Drue, who has owned it for seven years. It is hugely comfortable and attractive inside. Our stately bedroom has three large windows facing the lake and two side ones looking out to steep small mountains.

* * *

Sunny in late morning; in mid-afternoon it became cloudy and humid, followed by a few spots of light rain. We went to look at the Heinz aviary, a nice airy flight for a few doves, finches, small parrots and a grassy parade-ground for bantam hens. Discovered that the cockerel sounds I heard this morning, which I reckoned were a long distance off, came from here and ricocheted off the stone hillside.

Breakfast talk, between Natasha, Dr Casey and me (the others not being down, or had already been down) was mostly of T. S. Eliot, Waugh and Powell. I queried if the Sitwells were right in their assertion that Eliot, as a young man, used a pale green powder to make himself look more interesting. Natasha said Yes, he did, but I am dubious.

At lunch we were all together, out of doors. Drue and John Casey were brightly informative about travelling in the Yemen, Jack Profumo about various electronic and digital gadgets which he claims—wrongly I'm sure—not to understand. And Natasha gave a very sympathetic account of Aldous Huxley and his championship of mescalin in mushrooms. Over the years I have noticed, when eating delicious mushrooms, that as often as not Huxley's and Robert Graves's names will crop up.

Lovely scents released from the garden by the few spots of rain. Now it rains properly; the circular swimming-pool looks very wet and mountains and lake have disappeared.

Sunday 26 May
After dinner last night we watched a video of

'Princess Caraboo'. I was wearing neither my hearing-aid nor my distance glasses so I missed about 40 per cent. Outside it lashed with rain.

This morning was a little misty but by 09.30 the lake came into view and then the mountains. It became a superb day. We left from Cadenabbia on the ferry at 12.30, lunching on board and calling at Varenna, Menaggio, Bellano, Piona (of that in a moment) and Gravedona; then did the whole thing more or less in reverse, leaving out Menaggio but calling at Bellagio, where we disembarked for super ice-creams, lemonade, etc., sitting under trees at a waterside café. We were there for an hour and a half before catching another ferry back to Cadenabbia.

The idea had been to disembark at Piona—a tiny spot with a metal pier—to see the monastery. Natasha Spender and M, on her crutches, were ashore in a flash and the ferry pushed off without waiting for the rest of us to disembark. The trouble had been that Jack Profumo and I had been having a quite friendly altercation with the stewards about the luncheon bill; we maintaining it had been included in the fare and they denying it. They were right. By the time we had sorted things out and paid, Merula and Natasha were left lonely and alone on shore and we were heading for Gravedona. We found we were able to pick them up an hour later. They seemed to have enjoyed themselves; got to the monastery but found everything too crowded for comfort.

Bellagio, which is almost opposite Casa Ecco, is an attractive, busy little town with good shops as well as the frippery to catch the tourist eye. It looks prosperous, and on a Whit Sunday afternoon was crowded with Italian families with their happy, well-behaved children. The only unexpected note was struck by a group of Nordic-looking men, stripped to the waist and with gold rings through their nipples. All the places we put into on the northern shores of the lake were attractive looking, with their pale terracotta houses and tree-lined promenades, but the one I would like most to revisit—perhaps for a holiday—is Bellagio.

It being Sunday, the lake was patchily white with racing sailing-boats and innumerable sailboards, skimming on the water like greenish mayflies and dangerously cutting across the bows of the ferry. Most of them ended up flat on the water, their owners quite unperturbed.

After dinner (a vast goose egg each in a glorious sauce, followed by miraculous veal) we sat down in the drawing-room where the conversation was political and fascinating, conducted mostly by Lord Briggs, John Casey and Profumo. Even apolitical creatures like M and myself were spellbound. Lord Briggs was brilliant and warm-hearted, and Jack Profumo and John Casey equally vivid. It was well after midnight when we got to bed.

Monday 27 May
Thunder, lightning and heavy rain woke us in the early hours. Rain lessened but continued until elevenish. Drue arranged for a large motorboat to collect us at Tremezzo, a mile or two south, in mid-afternoon, and take us to Como. M took one look at the slight movement on the water and decided to return to Casa Ecco. Natasha didn't even contemplate the trip. It was all spectacularly beautiful, skimming over blue water, past fine villas and wooded mountains rising dramatically on either side. It took about an hour and forty minutes to reach Como, which was crowded. We indulged ourselves, sitting outside a café in the Cathedral piazza, with very elaborate ice-creams or a cappuccino or two. There was a long slow queue for the café's loo.

The facade of the Cathedral is striking but I found the inside rather heavy and gloomy. Yesterday Valerie lost a precious silk sunshade, so candles were lit invoking St Anthony and his remarkable ability to find things. Needless to say when we got home this evening the parasol had been found. St Anthony is very exacting and I am sure Valerie will reward his poor box handsomely.

Many years ago, before I became a Catholic, I wandered one day into Brompton Oratory. Spotting a little screw of paper lying at the feet of a statue to St A, I was inquisitive to know what might be written on it. 'Please, St Anthony, help me find my handbag', perhaps; or 'Where did I drop my penknife?' I looked round furtively to make sure I wasn't being watched and then unfolded the paper. I read it, refolded it and gave it back to the statue. Any superior smile had been wiped off my face. What I had read was very simple: 'Please, St Anthony, help me to find work.'

Sadly Lord B left for England this morning and chit-chat this evening was mostly ecclesiastical, with me holding forth interminably with tales of various popes and Leonard Cheshire *et al.* The others must have got very anxious, wondering if I would ever stop. I had had only one Campari (admittedly strong) before dinner and one glass of white wine with my fish, so I don't think my garrulousness can be laid at an alcoholic door. Age and the compulsion to reminisce, I fear. If only I would cut my anecdotes in half, not spend such unnecessary time setting the scene in a theatrical way and get to the point swiftly and clearly, I could save myself and others a lot of embarrassment.

Probably it would be better not to speak at all, keep lips sealed like Lord Baldwin or just offer Yea for Yea and Nay for Nay. There are times when I fear an almost catatonic silence has gripped me and I take a heedless plunge to break it.

Tuesday 28 May
Gloriously sunny all day but the wind has been violent and sometimes chilly. White horses breaking on the lake, the ferry and small boats chugging into them with determination. Glad we did our Como visit yesterday.

We all set off at noon for Menaggio, where we spent an hour. M and I visited the dark, cool, quiet and not very interesting church (so far as we could see) while the others shopped—Drue and Valerie gravitate to most shop-windows. Susan Briggs and Jack busied themselves with their cameras. Before we returned home we forgathered at a very nice café with a splendid view towards Bellagio and had Campari sodas.

Lunched out of doors at the villa, holding on with one hand to hats, table-mats and anything else likely to fly away while forking marvellous spaghetti with the other. Scratchy patches of snow could be seen on the mountains opposite and as lunch ended I felt the need to dress up as Scott or Shackleton. M spent a couple of hours in a sheltered spot drawing. The aviary beckoned me and I spent some time whistling to the birds before having a long, late siesta.

Drue was in rattling good form after dinner and kept us highly entertained with tales about the much-loved parrot she once had. We talked of birds we have loved or encountered.

Alas, tomorrow Drue and Susan Briggs have to return to England, leaving the Profumos, Natasha Spender, M and me to our own devices.

Wednesday 29 May
A perfect day: warm sun and a gentle cool breeze. The scent of box is pervasive. Tiny lizards, possibly recently hatched, scampered over the pinkish-beige gravel paths; birdsong and bantam cock-crow filled the air. The lake and mountains were sharply defined. I must be careful not to form too great an attachment to this form of life.

Drue and Susan Briggs left after breakfast, heading for Milan airport and London. I don't know how Drue can bear to leave this place, but her energy spreads far and wide and she has a thousand enterprises to see to. When Natasha leaves tomorrow there will be only the Profumos and ourselves until we all go on Saturday. I had suggested to Drue that we should leave with her but she wouldn't hear of it.

Merula spent much of morning and afternoon sketching; Jack went to local village to buy bathing trunks—with which he is highly delighted—and I ensconced myself in the gazebo, which I have more or less purloined as my private territory.

So far I've only achieved about twenty pages of my much vaunted assault on *Copperfield*. The trouble is not *Copperfield*, which is gloriously rewarding, but the unexpected and unusual books that catch one's eyes. As soon as Natasha has put it down I'm going to make a snatch at *Culture of Complaint* by Robert Hughes. I shall be unable to finish it before we leave but shall order a copy when we get home. Just the introduction makes me know it will intrigue.

During and after dinner Jack Profumo kept us enthralled with appraisals and anecdotes of wartime (39/45) military leaders. Valerie expressed hero-worship for Montgomery, whom she had found warm-hearted, charming and marvellous with her children. My own appraisal was of a vain actor playing to the gallery, brilliant, of course, but somehow offputting. I thought, in the social circumstances, it would be sensible to keep my ignorance to myself.

Thursday 30 May
While sitting in the gazebo my diuretic pill caught me unawares in a very imperative way. Too far to get back safely to the house. Oh, Lord, I do hope I haven't withered a box hedge.

It is another summer day. Everything more than a hundred yards away looks quite hazy, the mountains appear soft and Lake Como a pale grey-blue smudge. M is proud of herself, having just circumnavigated the stone walls of the property, which must have taken her quite a time on her crutches. There is no question that she looks rested and altogether better, but I long for the day when she can throw away all aids to walking: it is now over seven months since her hip-replacement operation.

This house is stuffed with books, most libraried but a lot scattered casually to entice guests. This morning I noticed the Barry Humphries novel I so enjoyed recently, and I remembered John Casey telling two connected stories concerning Humphries. The first one was of a Cambridge don who said he had just seen on TV a remarkable woman called Dame Edna Everage. He said he had agreed with every word she had said and he considered her the most sensible woman he had ever seen on the box. The second one concerned the father of a Cambridge Fellow who, when his son went to visit the old gentleman, greeted him with 'I have been looking at the most disgustingly awful programme on TV it has been my misfortune ever to see. A totally loathsome man. You really would think that the Australian Government should be able to find a more suitable cultural attaché than this ghastly Les Patterson.'

Tonight we are venturing out to dinner to a highly acclaimed little restaurant ten minutes away where they specialize in rabbit dishes.

M and I don't much like rabbit but presumably there will be alternative things to eat. In any case it will give a little respite to Drue's hard-working and adorable staff.

Friday 31 May
The roast rabbit was probably excellent but didn't convert me to rabbit eating. The sauce was good but I don't like all those little bones which might belong to a baby's fingers. We liked the trattoria, called Fagurido, about two miles away and beautifully situated high up among trees, through which we had a fine view of the lake. It was a warm evening so we had our meal out of doors on a wooden terrace. There were no other customers. The sweet girl who served looked remarkably like Geraldine Chaplin, which added to the prettiness of things. The moon was nearly full and as lights came on, one by one, in the mountain villages, their reflections dropped straight as rulers across the water.

I spoke to Mrs Spurdle before going out and she said England has had its hottest day this year.

This morning is perfection, hot and hazy, with air like cool carbonated water. M has been for a bit of a walk along grassy paths winding up behind the house and has now settled down to her stitch-work. The Profumos have gone shopping in Menaggio. What I would really like to do this afternoon is to take a boat to Bellagio to have a look around but I don't want to cause inconvenience. I know that Paul, Drue's young driver, would show total willingness but I feel he should have time to himself; tomorrow he drives the four of us to Milan and then immediately sets out on his sixteen-hour car journey back to England.

*   *   *

In luck; Paul announced that he was going over to Bellagio at three and did any of us wish to join him. Jack and I jumped at it; the ladies settled for a quiet life at home. It is 82 and proved rather too hot for climbing cobbled steps. The shops were mostly the usual tourist boutiques. The other day I spotted a shop there which looked as if it might have something to appeal to M and today I made straight for it. Everything it had was heavy knitted or crocheted wool; stuff I didn't even want to look at, let alone handle, the temperature being what it is.

The only English I heard spoken in Bellagio was from a youngish American couple and also from two elderly Scottish ladies. The Americans were discussing the merits of cars on the ferry while licking chocolate ice-cream cones and catching each other's eyes in a suggestive way. The Scottish ladies spent minutes gazing, with canny looks, at a cluster of teaspoons in a silversmith's:

'Are they genuine, would you say?' one said.

'We'll ask Ada, she'll know,' said the other, turning round to look for Ada, but no Ada was to be seen. Consternation.

Back at the villa by five in time to see Merula swinging off on her crutches up a fairly gentle hillside. I decided on an hour's sticky lie-down and then a cool bath.

Dinner on the terrace was dream-like. All was still, quiet and pale blue except for candlelight and fireflies exploding into brilliance against the cypress trees. It has been a fitting last evening to a blissful holiday.

JUNE 1996

Sunday 2 June
We set off for Milan at 12.45 yesterday, Paul driving beautifully and keeping up an amusing East London commentary, but never too much. It had been arranged that wheelchairs would be at the airport for Valerie and Merula but no, we had to go to a sort of Black Hole of Calcutta or Sartre's Huis Clos, and wait for two hours for wheelchairs to arrive, breathing carefully in an airless 84°. The airport was in a state of chaos and misinformation. Our BA flight was an hour late. We were shamed in our impatience by a small group of English ladies who had been on a tour of Egypt, Israel, Greece and Italy. They were enthusiastic about everything except Bethlehem.

'Very disappointing, Bethlehem. Not at all like they told us in Bible class. Still, you have to remember it was all two thousand years ago. No shepherds looking after their flocks now; no grass; just lots and lots of little houses. Always wanted to see the pyramids and now I've done it. *They* look just as they do in the pictures.'

We were home by 19.30 Saturday, tired but happy. Joyous greeting from the dogs. Early to bed. Merula accidentally left her crutches behind at Casa Ecco. It could be, of course, a

267

sort of psychological miracle. They will be delivered to London in a day or two.

Today has been one of unpacking, wonderment at how the trees have spread their leaves in our short absence, telephoning friends and avoiding the pile of letters to be answered.

Monday 3 June
The Welsh National Opera presented *Nabucco* from Cardiff on BBC2 TV last night, Sunday. A good sing-along but I didn't care for the minimalist setting (mostly something that looked like a static escalator) and I was very doubtful about the Holocaust-like interpretation. I do wish people would write their own plays or musicals on subjects that appeal to them and not twist the classics. I saw it all except for the few minutes when Peter Glenville telephoned from New York. He sounded chirpy and when I asked, rather gravely, after his health, which has been causing anxiety, he laughed, saying, 'That's the first time I have heard you sound *old*. I'm fine but haven't a lot of energy. Going to the hospital in Houston on Friday for a check-up and then on to Mexico. Hope to come to England in September. See you then.'

* * *

(Later: nearly midnight. Still Monday.)

An hour ago, while reading in bed, I heard the telephone and Alan, who was in my study, answer it. I assumed it was a call for him. He came upstairs to tell me that it had been Marguerite Littman and gently broke the news that Peter had died in the night. A heart attack. It must have been a few hours after he had telephoned. For me, after a close friendship of over fifty years, that is a considerable full stop.

Tuesday 4 June
The morning was taken up with telephone calls in connection with Peter's death and trying to arrange a Requiem Mass for him in London. The trouble is that there can be only a handful of his English friends still alive. I spoke to Marguerite Littman again, to Drue and Laurence Evans. Finally I tracked down Fr. Philip Caraman sj at his parish in Somerset. Peter and Fr. Caraman were boys together at Stonyhurst and kept contact throughout life. I suggested the Mass should be said at the Oratory, which was Peter's local church for many years, and Philip offered to officiate. We settled for Wednesday 26 June, if that is acceptable to the Oratory Fathers.

My mind remains numbly blank. And my heart, too, curiously enough. Sorrow will come for sure, in its own time and, I am sure, dozens of happy or absurdly funny memories; but for the moment all is grey, in spite of brilliant sunshine. I had hoped to complete this diary with no further obituaries but that was not to be. Sometime, somehow, I must try to write something about Peter. But not now.

Wednesday 5 June
A very hot cloudless day. The fish were frantic for food at eight. The brown woolly lamb in the paddock, who has taken a fancy to Alan Bennett, didn't come to his usual corner of the fence to have his head scratched but kept his distance in a bit of shade.

Up in town by 11.45. Sent David Pike back with M's crutches, left at Como and kindly brought back by Paul the chauffeur and left at the Connaught. To my bank to change lire into sterling and was delighted to find I was given a much bigger lump of cash than expected. That went dizzily to my head so I lunched at Wiltons, bought a nightshirt at Turnbull & Asser and then on to the Japanese shop, Miyake, in Fulham Road to buy M a rather odd but attractive scarf—silk, sage green and looking like a fishing net.

In late afternoon to see Fr. Michael Hollings at St Mary of the Angels in Bayswater. He lives in the parish house, which was built by Cardinal Manning, next to the church. It is a ramshackle place with innumerable rooms and divided staircases but with an atmosphere quite out of the ordinary. A half-naked young man was slumped, either drunk or drugged, on the hallway stairs. No one paid the slightest attention to him—he was probably an habitué—just skirted round him without comment. He had chosen the coolest spot in London in which to pass out.

In the evening to Farm Street for the vigil Mass of Corpus Christi, a feast I always like.

Laurie Evans and his wife Mary joined me for dinner. Laurie was my agent for about thirteen years after the war; then we fell out over negotiations for a film I choose to forget. However, all was well. The Evanses were good friends of Peter G so our evening was full of reminiscences, some of them very funny, and mostly about Peter, Terence Rattigan and Binkie Beaumont; all gone now and all exceedingly good company. One of the surprising qualities Peter possessed was great physical bravery; he seemed to be unaware of fear. Laurie is partly deaf, I wasn't wearing my hearing-aid, and so Mary had to bawl at each of us to keep the conversation comprehensible.

Speaking of the hard-of-hearing, or of the audibly deprived (I'm not sure of the politically correct term), Merula's hearing is declining, I fear. This morning I shouted across the lawn to her, 'You haven't forgotten tomorrow is Matthew's birthday, have you?' 'No,' she said, 'I shall be there at about seven o'clock.' It seemed pointless to pursue it further so I left for London.

Thursday 6 June

It is my dear Matthew's birthday, fifty-six today. He was born in the hospital at Denmark Hill. Merula had a rather beastly time and was very cross about the whole experience for quite a few days. I saw him first between a matinée and evening performance of *The Tempest* at the Old Vic in which Gielgud was playing Prospero, Jack Hawkins Caliban—one of the best ever—and I was Ferdinand, wearing a dazzling white costume designed by Oliver Messel which had a great Elizabethan ruff made out of pipe-cleaners. It looked marvellous but was hell to wear, the pipe-cleaners always getting bent or falling off. The wartime tram trips to Denmark Hill were time-consuming and fretful—but we had a son in whom we rejoiced. What more could a young couple ask? Except a little cash. My Old Vic salary was £12 a week.

The temperature in London has been 84. I went to Issey Miyake again to get a shirt for Matthew. Then to the House of Roux (sounds like a ladies' dress shop) where I got excellent raspberries, tasteless strawberries and an apricot flan. David Pike collected me at 11.30 and I was home in time for a late-ish lunch with M, Matthew and his girlfriend. We ate in the semi-shade of the patio, lightly and happily. M seems to like her fish-net scarf.

For several weeks I have known I wished to

finish this diary on 6 June but don't know why. Matthew coming into the world all that time ago, perhaps, which was an emotional experience; or possibly the Normandy Invasion, which signalled the beginning of the end of six years of war. I wasn't involved in Normandy but in the invasions of Sicily and Italy, which was really the start of the defeat of the Axis powers; Rome fell to the Allies a few days before our troops invaded France on June 6. In any case, it has always been a date firmly fixed in my mind.

The heat, shopping and travelling have worn me to a ravelling but at least I think I know how I wish to finish this off.

In Beatrix Potter's *The Tailor of Gloucester* the mice, who have been saved by the tailor from the wicked schemes of the cat Simpkin, set about sewing the buttonholes on the waistcoat being made for the Mayor of Gloucester, which is behindhand. Working on the last buttonhole they run out of thread. They leave a note of explanation in tiny writing:

No more twist.